OUTDOOR SAFETY&
SURVIVAL

OUTDOOR SAFETY & SURVIVAL

Revised and updated by

Judi Lees

GREYSTONE BOOKS

Douglas & McIntyre

Vancouver/Toronto

97 98 99 00 01   5 4 3 2 1

Revised edition

Greystone Books
A division of Douglas & McIntyre Ltd.
1615 Venables Street
Vancouver, British Columbia
V5L 2H1

CANADIAN CATALOGUING IN PUBLICATION DATA

Main entry under title:
Outdoor safety and survival

  Includes bibliographical references and index.
  ISBN 1-55054-569-8
  1. Wilderness survival. 2. Outdoor recreation—Safety measures.
GV200.5.O97 1997   613.6'9   C97-910006-2

Cover design by Kari McKinley/Hoy Jacobsen and Co. Inc.
Illustrations of plants by Nadaleen Tempelman-Kluit
Printed and bound in Canada by Best Book Manufacturers

The publisher gratefully acknowledges the assistance of the Canada Council and of the British Columbia Ministry of Tourism, Small Business and Culture.

CONTENTS

ACKNOWLEDGEMENTS

The information in this book was compiled with the assistance of many experts and skilled outdoorspeople. With thanks to Jim Allman, Emile Begin, Helen Metcalfe, Lorraine Methot, Gary Miltenberger, Karl Wagner and Whitney Numan, Ministry of Forests; Bridget Milsom, St. John Ambulance; Dr. Nancy J. Turner, University of Victoria; Dr. David Cox, Simon Fraser University, Bruce Wilson, H20 Mtn. Leadership School; Dr. Dirk Tempelman-Kluit; Mike Barker, Carly Haddon, Mountain Equipment Co-Op.

INTRODUCTION

This book is a guide to outdoor safety. It is designed to be read when you receive it and again when you are planning an outdoor trip. Carry it on your journey. Good outdoor survival information is as valuable as your food supply and first-aid kit.

Even the most experienced outdoorsperson can be caught in an emergency. Carefully preparing for a trip, understanding the outdoors, acknowledging your limitations and having a reliable source of information will give you the knowledge and self-confidence you will need if you are lost or injured in the wilderness.

The information in *Outdoor Safety and Survival* has been gleaned from experts with dozens of years of outdoor experience. Should an emergency occur, this guide will assist you in recognizing your situation and planning the next step.

Keep in mind that this book is not a substitute for survival training or a first-aid course—both are highly recommended.

1 <u>SURVIVAL PSYCHOLOGY</u>

We have all heard stories about people who have survived in crisis situations against insurmountable odds. Their "will to live," their determination to continue when a situation looked difficult and their belief in themselves are often cited as reasons that they survived.

When dealing with a crisis situation, you have a physiological and a psychological response. Physiologically, you may experience an adrenaline rush and an increase in blood pressure, you may perspire, and your muscles may tighten. Psychologically, you may lose your ability to focus, you may become indecisive, and you may experience a feeling of helplessness. Although all of these are normal reactions to stress, they have to be overcome.

A threatening situation often elicits a "fight or flight" response. The "fight" response means facing up to your situation. Don't let the crisis immobilize you; focus on what you have to do to survive. It is imperative to use your energy in a positive way. You would not choose to be in this situation, but you are. Accept the challenge.

In order to "fight," recognize the problems that you may face.

PROBLEMS TO OVERCOME

1. **Fear.** Fear is a normal reaction. To prevent your fear from turning into panic, some survival courses advocate that the first thing to do when you are lost, stranded or injured in the wilderness is STOP: Sit, Think, Observe and Plan. When you feel yourself beginning to panic, remember the acronym STOP. Once you have a plan, you have something to do, and action is an excellent antidote to fear (see chapter 5).

2. **Pain.** Pain is your body's way of making you pay attention to something that is wrong. In a survival situation, pain may go unnoticed if your mind is kept occupied with plans for

survival. Although pain can often be tolerated, it is important that you treat any injury immediately (see chapter 16).

3. **Cold.** Dealing with the cold may be one of your biggest challenges. If you have prepared well for your trip, you can take heart that you have the proper clothing and equipment. To warm your body, move your large-muscle groups. Gathering firewood, for example, will help you warm up. Taking action also gives you confidence in your ability to look after yourself.

4. **Thirst.** As with pain, you can ignore thirst if you are concentrating on surviving. But ignoring thirst can lead to dehydration. Acquiring a source of water is an important part of your survival plan. Knowing how to find and purify water (see chapter 8) will give you confidence and keep you healthy. Should you be short of water, cut down on your food intake and use the information in chapter 8 about how to obtain water.

5. **Hunger.** It is heartening to realize that if you are in good physical condition, you can survive several weeks without food as long as you have water. We are conditioned to eating on a schedule, however, and you require food for warmth and energy. Finding and preparing food is important. When you first realize that you are lost, give your body some nourishment. Making yourself a warm drink after you have a fire started will give you confidence that you are looking after yourself and taking control of the situation. Once you are settled into your camp, look at all your options for acquiring food (see chapters 9 and 10).

6. **Fatigue.** Because it is almost impossible to avoid some degree of fatigue, it is necessary to understand its effects and allow for them. In a survival situation, you get less food and sleep. But you may also use fatigue as an escape from a difficult situation. Recognize these dangers and combat them. Take care of yourself by resting and avoiding too much physical exertion. Always look at energy-saving methods of doing a

chore. For example, when you are building a shelter, choose the one you feel you have the strength to build. Don't give in to mental fatigue—have a goal, even if it is simply to stock firewood.

7. **Boredom and loneliness.** Although often unexpected, boredom and loneliness are two tough enemies. While you are waiting for help, boredom may sneak up on you, accompanied by depression. To overcome boredom and to avoid feelings of loneliness, keep yourself busy—make your camp comfortable, prepare signals for Search and Rescue, and investigate food possibilities.

TO SURVIVE

1. Recognize that survival may depend more on your outlook than on weather, terrain or the nature of the emergency.

2. Realize that you have choices—you can improvise, you can be creative, and you have the skills to survive a difficult situation.

3. Set goals. Your short-term goals are to obtain shelter, warmth, water and food. Your long-term goal is to be found, so prepare ground signals and always have three fires ready to set should you see or hear an aircraft (see chapter 14).

4. Don't be fooled by thinking that "it can't happen to me." Equip yourself with the skills and the proper mental attitude so that if a crisis occurs you will survive.

2 <u>BEFORE YOUR TRIP</u>

Before taking a trip into the wilderness, leave detailed information about your outing with a responsible person. This information should include where you are going and what route you intend to follow; how you are getting to the trailhead and where you plan to leave your vehicle; how long you will be gone; what the purpose of your trip is—for example, hiking, fishing or canoeing; how many people are in your party; and what type of supplies you have taken (for example, if you have a first-aid kit, signalling device and emergency food). Do not hike alone.

If a party does not return from a wilderness trip when expected, the police should be notified. It is the police who contact Search and Rescue.

In preparation for the trip, make a list of the clothing and equipment you will need and tick off items as you pack them. Make sure that you are adept at using all of your equipment. No matter how short a trip you are taking into the backcountry, always carry the basics: map, matches or lighter, flashlight, knife, plastic sheet or space blanket, extra clothing, whistle, water and emergency food.

Experience and outdoor skills are invaluable. For information about wilderness survival courses or first-aid training, contact:

Federation of Mountain Clubs of BC
#336-1367 W. Broadway
Vancouver, BC V6H 4A9
Tel: 737-3166; outside the Lower Mainland, 1-800-298-9919

For information on wilderness first aid, contact:

St. John Ambulance
6111 Cambie St.

Vancouver, BC V5Z 3B2
Tel: 321-2651

This is the provincial headquarters. In other areas, the organization is listed in the phone book.

3 <u>CLOTHING and EQUIPMENT</u>

CLOTHING

How well you are dressed plays a big part in survival. Clothing must offer protection from the elements, be comfortable and not hamper movement; stiff, heavy clothes, such as denim jeans, tire you out quickly when you are travelling. Over the years there have been great advances in the development of high-tech materials for outdoor clothing. Choose wisely for the conditions.

In winter

Wear clothing that will retain body heat yet allow body moisture to evaporate. Dressing in layers is an effective method of maintaining a healthy body temperature. Your goal is to prevent a cold, clammy buildup of moisture inside your clothing. The layers act as pathways that transport sweat away from the skin to the outside; as the body heats, layers can be removed.

In cold weather the first layer should be a mid-weight polyester fabric designed to wick moisture away from your body. Unlike cotton, polyester does not absorb moisture. (Hint: Shaking out polyester is a great way to speed up drying.) For extreme cold, wear heavier knit underwear.

The next upper-body layers should be a combination of fabrics such as wool and fleece—for example, a wool turtleneck and a fleece vest. (A vest keeps the body core warm and permits your arms to move freely.) Wool insulates better than any other natural fabric; avoid cotton, which absorbs moisture and loses its insulating qualities when wet. Fleece is a polyester fabric that is comfortable, absorbs little moisture, dries quickly and insulates.

The outer layer should be as waterproof as possible. There are a number of waterproof, breathable fabrics that stop moisture from entering and allow sweat to leave. The best known of these is Gore-Tex, and there is a variety of jacket styles to choose from.

On the lower part of your body, if the weather is not wet, wear a pant of mid-weight fleece ("200" fleece is medium weight) with side zippers to help regulate body temperature. If it is not windy, nylon-shelled fleece is a good choice. For rain or wet snow, wear waterproof pants over layers of underwear and fleece; wool pants are another alternative, but they are itchy.

Winter clothing is designed with fastenings at the neck, waist, sleeve and ankle to be adjusted as your body warms or cools.

From 20 to 50 per cent of your body heat can be lost through your head. Wear a waterproof, wool-lined hat that wraps under your chin. A woollen toque is fine in dry cold but absorbs rain and snow.

There are many choices for keeping your hands warm. Although mittens limit manual dexterity, it is generally agreed that they keep hands warmer than gloves. As insulating materials improve, however, this distinction is becoming less important. The layering system applies to hands as well. Combine a tightly fit, liner glove (wool, fleece or some other type of polyester) over a water-resistant outer mitt. The outer mitt should tighten above the wrist to form an overlapping barrier with your jacket sleeve. This barrier prevents snow and rain from getting to your liner and freezing your fingers. The outer mitt should have an abrasion-resistant coated palm.

In extreme conditions, your body services the brain and central nervous system first. Your feet are the first to suffer from lack of circulation. Wear a sock liner that has a blend of fabrics designed to wick moisture and provide warmth. Wear one or two pairs of socks over the liner. There is a wide choice of mountaineering socks to choose from; some people still prefer wool. Wool blended with a synthetic is more durable.

For winter, a leather, Gore-Tex-lined boot will keep your feet warm and dry. If you wear leather boots, apply waterproofing treatment regularly. There are also water-repellent nylon or nylon-leather boots, which are less water-resistant. Wear boots that have been well broken in. Most have several insoles, which can be removed if they become damp. Pull sock tops inside your pants, make sure that there are no wrinkles in your socks, and do not lace boots too tightly. Good flow of blood is mandatory for warm feet.

Hint: When fitting boots, gloves, mittens and even your sleeping bag, always make sure that there is room between your body and the insulating material—for example, in boots there must be room to wiggle your toes but not enough to allow your foot to move. If you do not have this extra space, you are packing down the insulation, and it loses its heat-retaining quality.

Sunglasses with UV-protection lenses and durable frames will reduce fatigue and prevent eye damage. In winter, snow blindness is a concern. In an emergency, goggles can be made from a piece of bark (birch works well) cut with small slits and held on by rope tied to each end.

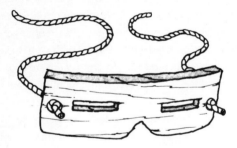

In summer
Since nights in the mountains can be chilly, dress in layers. Always carry a rain jacket and an extra layer of warmth, such as a fleece jacket or vest, in your backpack in case the weather changes.

On warm days wear cotton or nylon-blend shorts or long pants. There is a nylon pant or short that comes with elasticized waist, several pockets with Velcro closings and knit cuffs on the pant legs. Hiking shirts of polyester/nylon blends are comfortable. Keep in mind that pants with cuffs and long-sleeved shirts are good bug and sun barriers. Combine a lightweight fleece top with a windproof, water-repellent shell. Wear a hat for sun and rain protection—a wide-brimmed canvas one that ties on is one example. Wear securely fastened sunglasses.

All clothing should fit loosely—it should have an elasticized waist and should include wide-legged pants and a loose-fitting shirt, sweater and jacket. Loose clothing permits air to circulate when it is hot yet gives you layers when it cools off later in the day.

EQUIPMENT

The amount of equipment you'll require depends on the length of your trip and the type of country you are travelling in. Certain items should always be carried, however, either in your pockets or in an easily accessible pouch. Besides ensuring that you are ready for any emergency, the equipment you carry should make your trip easier and more comfortable.

Suggested equipment to carry in your pockets

- **Fire starter.** Waterproof matches. You can waterproof ordinary matches by dipping the heads into melted candle wax or nail polish. A butane lighter is an excellent fire starter.
- **Pocketknife.** Equipped with sharp blade, awl and screwdriver.
- **Sunglasses or goggles**
- **Compass.** With high-grade steel needles that rotate on precision bearings; should be liquid filled and have a luminous button.
- **Map.** Topographical map of area.
- **Notebook and pencil.** For recording information such as landmarks and observations made during the journey and for leaving a message should you be forced to abandon camp.

- **Trail food.** For example, nuts, raisins, energy bars, or fruit leather.
- **Bandanna.** Handy for washing your face, tying around your head to keep sweat off and many other uses.
- **Space blanket or piece of plastic sheeting**
- **Whistle.** On a shoelace so that it can be worn around the neck. Use a plastic whistle if temperatures are below freezing.
- **Sunscreen**
- **Emergency first-aid materials, such as Band-Aids**

Survival kit

The recommended survival kit is packed in a lightweight, water-tight metal container measuring about 10 cm by 13 cm. It can be attached to your belt and can be used as a cooking pot. It should be sealed with vinyl tape. If you fall into water, you may have to discard your backpack, but you will have your survival kit. Contents vary and some people will choose to carry specific items in their pockets, as listed above, whereas others will have them in the survival kit. Suggested items are:

1. **Medicine kit.** First-aid supplies should be packed in air-tight containers with cotton wool. Everything should be labelled with the dosage, expiry date and instructions. Do not take pills with alcohol. The kit should contain:
   - Analgesic such as Tylenol to relieve moderate pain
   - Antihistamine to relieve allergies, insect bites and stings
   - Diarrhea suppressant
   - Antacid for upset stomach
   - Water-sterilizing tablets
   - Variety of bandages—medium compress bandage, several small compress bandages, butterfly sutures (which pull edges of wound together), several large Band-Aids and five small Band-Aids

2. **Food**
   - An instant drink that replenishes salt
   - Dehydrated meat
   - Soups—chicken and beef
   - Ingredients for hot drinks—tea bags, coffee, sugar
   - Juice mix
   - Energy bars
3. **Waterproof matches or matches in waterproof container.** (Remember to have striker, such as a piece of sandpaper.)
4. **Solid fuel to be used when wood is wet**
5. **Signalling mirror**
6. **Fluorescent strip of marker panel** (about 2 m x .3 m) to signal for help
7. **Signal flares** to attract attention; can also be used to start a fire
8. **Aluminum pot that carries survival kit**
9. **Spoon**
10. **Knife.** In addition to a multibladed knife, take a general-purpose one that will assist with preparing food, even skinning animals. Blade should be protected by tape when you are travelling.
11. **Aluminum foil**
12. **Emergency saw**
13. **Nylon shroud cord,** about 6 m
14. **Fishing line,** 15 m
15. **Small fish hooks** (20)
16. **Medium fish hooks** (8)
17. **Compass**
18. **Whistle**
19. **Small flashlight**—make sure batteries are good
20. **Wire** for suspending cooking container
21. **Plastic bags** (2 large garbage bags and 2 small bags)
22. **Emergency blanket**—a waterproof, reflective blanket that helps retain body heat

23. **Snare wire**—8 m can be wrapped around knife
24. **Spare prescription eyeglasses,** if applicable
25. **Outdoor survival guide** that includes ground-to-air signals
26. **Biodegradable soap**—good for you and your dishes

First-aid kit

Wilderness first aid begins with a well-equipped kit and the knowledge of how to use it. In addition to the first-aid remedies contained in your survival kit, pack the following in a compact, sturdy, waterproof container. Remember to pack any medications required for personal medical problems, such as specific allergies.

- **Triangular bandages,** 1 or 2
- **Adhesive tape,** 5-cm roll, 2.5 cm wide
- **Band-Aids,** 6 for small lacerations
- **Sterile gauze pads,** 2 to 6, 10 cm square
- **Razor blade,** 1 single-edge for shaving hair away from wound
- **Needle,** 1 medium-size to remove splinters, etc.
- **Moleskin,** 1 to 2 packages for blisters
- **Tensor bandage,** 1, 7 cm, for sprains, applying pressure, etc.
- **Antiseptic solution** in plastic container (Povidone-iodine)
- **6 tsp each of salt and baking soda and 12 tsp of sugar** to make a fluid that assists with rehydration or shock

Backpacks

There is a wide variety of styles available in multi-day backpacks. When choosing a pack, consider the volume of what you need to carry. Rule of thumb is that a 65- to 75-L pack will do for a summer trip of up to five or six days or a two- to three-day winter excursion. For an extended winter trip, choose a 75- to 85-L backpack. Over 85 L is for a serious winter expedition. Made of a blend of hard-wearing fabrics, most multi-day backpacks have a built-in frame that fits snugly to your back. Some people still prefer a backpack with an external rigid frame, which looks bulky and old-fashioned, but it is efficient for carrying heavy loads. In an emergency, this kind of backpack can be used to transport an injured person.

When purchasing a backpack, choose the correct size. A pack should be the same length as your back—measure between the large bump at the back of your neck down to a point on your back that lines up with the top of your hip bone.

Loading your pack

Packing heavy items at the top and close to your body distributes the weight properly on your body. It is a good idea to pack your sleeping bag and infrequently used items on the bottom, cooking utensils and clothing in the middle, and stove and other heavy items at the top. Pack sharp, hard objects inside the load, where they will not rub against the pack. Frequently used articles should be in outside pockets or immediately under the flap, where they are easily accessible. Maps and other flat objects should be in the top flap pocket. If it's wet, place damp items in polythene bags.

For comfort and efficiency, adjust the straps so that you can move the top part of your body and swing your arms freely. It is important that shoulder straps be adjusted so that the frame is in the centre of your back, with the weight being borne on your hips. The hip belt should fit snugly on the top of your hip bones. When you are carrying a heavy load, the centre of gravity should be high.

Suggested equipment to carry
in your pack, vehicle or boat
- **Flashlight.** Small, two-cell light, extra batteries and bulb—batteries lose their charge quickly if not kept warm.
- **Extra jacket, shirt or sweater** for an extra layer
- **Extra inner soles**

- **Extra mittens**
- **Extra wool socks.** Light, medium and heavy for changing into at night or when others get damp.
- **Spare large bandanna**
- **Pocket saw**
- **Fire starter.** Waterproof matches and butane lighter.
- **Tinder.** Anything that burns with a spark—for example, pine cones, bits of bark.
- **Small gas camp stove.** Avoid butane, since it will freeze.
- **Small first-aid kit**
- **Suncreen as well as ointment** in case of sunburn
- **Emergency food.** Extra supply of trail mix, soup mixes and bouillon cubes.
- **Avalanche cord.** Roll of 15-m to 22-m heavy cotton red string with directional arrows.
- **Sleeping bag.** There is a variety of styles and fillings. For cold, dry weather, a down-filled bag is warmest. In a wet climate, however, synthetic fillings are better, since they dry much faster. (Synthetic fibres break down over time; down does not.) Choose the thickness ("loft") of the bag according to the conditions you will be in. A bag rated for 10°C will not keep you warm at –20° C. A Polarguard is the heaviest and thickest synthetic-filled bag.

  Sleeping bags come in a "mummy" style, which has less space around your body and therefore retains more heat. A barrel-shaped bag has more space but is less heat efficient. Some sleeping bags have a neck baffle, which helps keep you warm. When purchasing a sleeping bag, remember that the less zipper area, the greater the heat retention.
- **Sleeping pads.** For the best and warmest sleep, choose a self-inflatable pad filled with foam. It rolls into a small shape and is inflated by opening the valve. Do not blow air into the valve or you will introduce moisture. When deflating the pad, roll from the end opposite to the valve. Choose a standard

pad over the one with the rippled finish, since the ⌐
breaks down more quickly. There are also foam insulate
pads, which protect you from the cold but are not comfortable.

- **Tent.** A tent is an instant shelter from the weather and must
  be chosen carefully. A free-standing tent is easy and quick to
  assemble and compact to store. It's a good idea to choose one
  with a vestibule for storing and keeping your gear dry. The
  more pole intersections, the more stable the tent. Smaller
  panels provide better wind resistance. For snowy conditions,
  the more vertical the wall, the better. If you don't have a tent
  on a day trip, always carry a large sheet of plastic to make a
  shelter.

The above equipment will ensure your comfort and safety if
you run into bad weather or if your trip is delayed for another
reason.

tter

UR COMPASS

The magnetic Silva-type compass is the oldest and most common direction-finding instrument. It is made up of four components:

1. A base plate to mark your line of travel
2. An adjustable ring marked off in 2-degree increments
3. A needle within this ring that points to magnetic north
4. A painted needle to adjust the difference between magnetic north and true north

The angle of difference between true north and magnetic north is called declination. You must always compensate for declination because all maps are made using true north. In British Columbia the range of declination is between 18 and 28 degrees. For example, in the southern coast region the compass reads about 22 degrees east of true north; near the B.C./Yukon border the declination is 28 degrees east.

Always hold the compass level and, especially in winter, allow ample time for the needle to finish its swing. It will do this slowly and sluggishly, but taking a bearing cannot be hurried if it is to be accurate.

Different compasses may require slightly different techniques to enable you to use them correctly—as an example, some compasses do not have a declination adjustment; others require a small screwdriver to make the adjustment. The following basic procedure will apply to all situations, however. After adjusting the declination, face the direction you want to go, extend your arm straight in front of you and aim the compass in this direction. Look over the top and centre of the compass and pick out a good landmark on this straight line—this is your sight line. Align the magnetic north arrow with the declination arrow in the adjustable ring. After the needle has stabilized and is in the middle of the painted arrow, check your landmark along your sight line. To determine what your direction of travel is, read the degree number on the outside of the adjustable ring. Record this reading (in case your adjustable ring should slip). Put your compass in your pocket and walk to this landmark. When you arrive there, take out your compass, line it up and aim as before, picking out a new landmark to head to on the same bearing. By repeating this whole sequence time after time, you will be able to proceed in a relatively straight direction. Example: Assume that you have decided to walk in a southeasterly direction, or about 135 degrees.

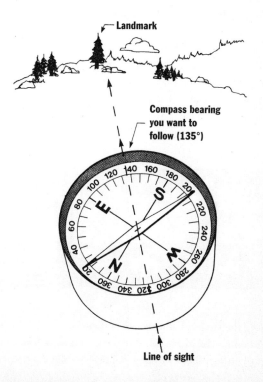

Landmark

Compass bearing you want to follow (135°)

Line of sight

USING A GLOBAL POSITIONING SYSTEM (GPS)

A GPS is a high-tech device that some outdoorspeople find invaluable. It is a hand-held instrument with digital readings that gathers information from satellites. It tells what your position is, which direction you are heading and how fast you are going, and it can plot a course. (There is a variety on the market, and they vary in what they can do.)

GPSS can be reliable and accurate, but since satellite information is periodically adjusted, the location accuracy can vary from day to day. (Some GPSS can make "real time" adjustments but are expensive.) Since GPSS run on batteries, you must carry extras for a long expedition (batteries last 4 to 12 hours). In addition, when you are in a narrow mountain valley, GPSS may be unable to read the satellite data, since they require readings from a minimum of three satellites.

OTHER WAYS OF FINDING DIRECTION

1. **Using the pole star.** To ascertain the pole star, find the Big Dipper or Plough—the two lowest stars in the Big Dipper point to the pole star. When you face the pole star, you are facing north.

2. **Using the sun and your watch.** Orient your watch by pointing the hour hand directly at the sun. Then by bisecting the angle between the hour hand and twelve o'clock, you have an

imaginary line running north and south. For example, at 8:00 A.M. it would appear thus:

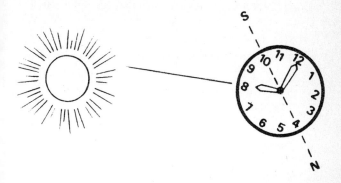

3. **Using your knife or a stick.** On overcast days when the sun is not visible, your knife (a small penknife will do) can assist you in finding your way. Hold the knife by the end of the handle. Stand the point on your thumbnail, rotate the knife slowly and watch for a faint shadow to be cast on the thumbnail. Rotate the blade to a position where the narrowest shadow is cast, the sun (hidden by clouds) is in the opposite direction of the shadow. Practise this technique before you need it so that you will have confidence in the reliability of this method.

4. **Using a camera light metre.** If you have a camera with a light metre, take a light-metre reading of the sky. The direction with the highest light reading is the location of the sun. The sun rises in the east and sets in the west. At mid-day in the Northern Hemisphere the sun is due south.

METHODS OF NAVIGATION

There are three common methods of getting from place to place:

1. **Map reading.** This is the most common method in developed countries. Both maps and air photos may be used.

When good landmarks exist, other instruments are generally not necessary.

2. **Map reading and compass combined.** This method requires the use of maps and air photos in conjunction with compass and distance-measuring devices.

3. **Dead reckoning.** This method is used in areas where landmarks are either inadequate or totally nonexistent—for instance, in dense forested areas, on the desert or on the Arctic barrens.

The first two methods are highly dangerous in areas where the terrain lacks distinctive features. The dead-reckoning method is recommended.

Navigation by dead reckoning

Dead reckoning consists of plotting and recording a series of courses, or "legs." The number of legs plotted depends on the length of the journey. Each is a straight line measuring the distance and direction from a known starting point. These connecting legs lead from the starting point to the destination. You work out each leg of the route and record them in pencil on the map. Then you are able to determine your position at any time either by following your plot or by comparing your actual position on the ground in relation to your plotted course.

Maps are used for selecting the route and also for plotting the actual route taken as the march progresses. As the navigator, you must know your starting point and objective, consult the map and decide on the best route, taking into consideration the terrain and the tactical situation. You also mark your progress on the map. Hint: Keeping your compass warm speeds up the taking of bearings.

When no aiming marks exist in front of you, use a landmark behind you as a bearing. Choose a landmark 180 degrees behind your line of sight and then swing around 180 degrees to establish your route of travel. You then check your travel based on the landmark behind you rather than one in front of you. Your aiming mark may be either some natural feature to your rear or an artificial aiming mark left behind by you, such as a cairn of rocks or a piece of material on a tree.

If the only aiming mark available is poorly defined—for example, a rock outcrop that has similar ones nearby—keep your eyes on it constantly after taking your bearing so that you don't lose it.

Never take bearings in the vicinity of metallic objects (such as watches, metal frames on glasses or firearms), since even a small amount of metal will affect your compass.

When visibility is poor, only close-by aiming marks will be available. Pick up further aiming marks frequently along the correct bearing. These marks should follow a straight line. Check your compass often to ensure that the correct bearing is being maintained.

Difficulties to overcome
The major difficulties in navigating in the wilderness are:

1. Lack of landmarks
2. Difficulty in judging distance because of lack of perspective and impaired visibility
3. Errors in distance measurements due to variation in pace length
4. Detours required to bypass obstacles

Remember, keep alert. Pay attention to the surrounding features of the land. Think of them as street signs. Your mental map of where you have been is based on what you see and notice along the way.

Your best navigational tools are your eyes, ears, nose and brain—when these are used efficiently with your map and compass, you will be able to travel from point A to point B and return.

5 <u>IF YOU GET LOST</u>

If you get lost in the wilderness, don't panic. Survival is a frame of mind. Fear of the unfamiliar and unknown weakens your ability to think and plan. This fear is only natural and can be expected. Keep in mind that although you cannot control your circumstances, you can control how you operate and live within them.

Your mind is your most powerful survival tool. A positive mental attitude is the result of the confidence that comes from experience, practice and eventual mastery of survival skills. It is also the result of choice. You can choose to make the most efficient use of what nature provides you with. You can also choose not to panic, to be calm and to assess the situation.

STOP
If you are lost, stranded or injured in the wilderness, STOP:

- Sit
- Think
- Observe
- Plan

TAKE IMMEDIATE ACTION
Make sure that you are in a safe setting—for example, not in danger from an avalanche or flash flood. Then use your first-aid kit to treat any injuries.

THINK BEFORE YOU ACT
AND CONSERVE YOUR STRENGTH
Emergency situations are never the same, and it is difficult to say that one step is more important than another. But your basic needs have to be met—heat, shelter, water and food as well as your emotional well-being. For some people, this last need may

be met by practising their faith; for other people, it may be met by gaining confidence as they manage to provide for themselves. How you go about meeting all these needs and what you do first will depend on the immediate environment and your physical and mental state.

BE CALM

Sit down, take a couple of deep breaths and try to relax. Think rationally. Write down how long it has been since you recognized a landmark. Consult your map and use your compass. It will help if you sketch out a rough map on paper or on the ground. You may find that you are lost only with regard to a trail or camp but can easily spot a landmark from which you can orient yourself.

ESTIMATE HOURS OF DAYLIGHT

To figure out how much daylight is left, face the sun, fully extend one of your arms towards the sun with your wrist bent inwards and your fingers just below the sun. Disregard your thumb and count how many finger widths separate the sun from the horizon. Allow 15 minutes per finger. Therefore, if four fingers fill the space between the horizon and the sun, sunset is an hour away.

KNOW THE PRIORITIES OF SURVIVAL

Shelter, water and fire are your first concerns. Whenever possible, choose a spot for a shelter well before dark. Pick a location away from natural hazards and, if possible, on high ground but out of the wind. It is advantageous to have a source of water nearby. Build a shelter, make a fire and have a snack and hot drink. At nightfall try to get a good night's sleep. Your situation may seem less intimidating when you are rested and have survived a night in the outdoors.

Assume that you are going to have a few days' wait for rescue and resist the urge to move in order to get home to family and friends. Spend your time wisely. It is best to keep your mind and body busy doing something productive. Find projects that do not require large outputs of energy. It is important to conserve your energy, but performing tasks will take your mind off your situation, help the time pass and reduce anxiety. You can:

1. Make your shelter as comfortable as possible.
2. Devise a means to carry and heat water to help keep you warm, hydrated and clean.
3. Set up some signals and have them ready for immediate use.
4. Gather firewood, food and water.
5. Relax and assess your situation.

Remember that cool, clear thinking will see you safely through the worst situations. Do not allow yourself to become rattled. If you find that you are half running and stumbling around, you are beginning to panic. STOP—Sit, Think, Observe, Plan.

Should you decide to move (see chapter 12), leave detailed markers, such as a forked branch stuck in the ground with another branch through it or rocks forming an arrow that points out the direction. These markers will also assist you if the direction you choose does not work out and you need to return to your original location. This starting point is your nearest known location to familiar surroundings. Always return to your original starting point before attempting a major change in course. Do not travel at night. Try to keep a fire burning; the smoke is a good signal during the day, and the flame shows up at night. If you have been lost 24 hours, rest assured that you will be looked for and that the search will centre on your last-known location.

6 BUILDING A FIRE

Fire is perhaps the most important single factor in successful survival. Without it, you will have a difficult time meeting your basic needs. It provides heat, purifies water, cooks foods, acts as a signal and helps dry clothing. When you are lost or confused, a fire will give you a psychological boost, help you relax and provide company on a cold, lonely night.

Fire is a great ally, but it is also an enormous responsibility when you are using it in the wilderness. A small fire, improperly set, can spread quickly, and soon a forest fire is burning out of control, causing additional problems.

FIVE COMMON MISTAKES IN LIGHTING A FIRE
1. Making a poor selection of tinder and fuel
2. Failing to shield the match or spark from the wind
3. Trying to light the fire from the downwind side
4. Using fuel that is damp or green
5. Smothering the newly lit fire with too much fuel or pieces that are too large

WHAT IS REQUIRED
Your first step is to plan your fire—the location and the materials required. A few extra minutes spent planning will save you time, energy and frustration later.

LOCATION OF THE FIRE
The ideal campfire site is on mineral soil, solid rock or a gravel bar. Forest fire hazard is always present with fires on muskeg, dry grass, leaves, evergreen needles or dead roots. A handy water supply or sand is useful for extinguishing flames.

Build your fire in an area where it can be easily spotted by a search-and-rescue team. If the ground is dry, scrape down to bare earth and clear an area before building your fire.

In winter, dig to solid ground, trample the snow or dig out an area around your shelter and fire area. If the snow is exceptionally deep, a small fire may be maintained by lighting it on top of a layer of green logs.

If possible, build your fire facing a large rock; the rock reflects heat and warms your body. A reflector can be added on the other side of the fire. It can be built of rocks in a horseshoe shape, or you can use a tent fly tied between two poles as a reflector. In addition, green or wet wood can be stacked as a reflector, and as the wood dries, it can be added to the fire.

Make sure the area above and all around your fire is clear of vegetation. Never build a fire against an old stump. Avoid building the fire in a depression because it will be difficult to burn long logs. If it is windy, however, dig a dish-shaped pit. If there are roots in the soil as you dig, line the entire pit with small stones. Do not use stones from a water course, since they may explode when heated.

Do not build a fire directly under a tree because there is a danger that snow may slide down from branches or that the dry humus and leaves may be ignited. The sequence of lighting a fire is spark, tinder, fuel, oxygen.

SPARK

Here are some of the most common methods of creating a spark.

1. **Matches**. These should be carried at all times when you are in the bush. Make sure that they are the "strike anywhere" type and that they are waterproof. You can make them waterproof by dipping each match into nail polish or melted paraffin. Store them in a waterproof container with a piece of sandpaper.

2. **A butane lighter**. This is an excellent source of spark. One that shows the amount of butane is best. Make sure that it is

packed in your survival kit in such a way that the gas-release button cannot be accidentally pressed. If you run out of butane, save the flint since it can still be a source of spark.

3. **Flint and steel**. This is one of the oldest methods of starting a fire. A flint-and-steel kit consists of a piece of flint rock, a striker and a piece of charred cotton cloth. Sparks created when you hit the metal striker with the flint should be directed onto the char cloth. Have fine, dry tinder ready. Cold wet weather does not affect the flint-and-steel method, but make sure that you have practised this method before relying on it in the bush. It is not easy to do.

4. **Battery**. A battery from a car, snowmobile, boat or airplane can produce an electric spark. Attach wires to each battery pole and scratch them together. Aim the spark produced at a rag dampened lightly with gasoline. Don't do this near your fuel supply.

5. **Spark plugs**. Spark plugs from a chain saw or outboard motor can produce a spark. Unscrew the spark plug but reconnect it to the plug wire. Place the plug on tinder that has a bit of gasoline on it; pull the starter cord.

6. **Ammunition**. Ammunition can be used to produce a spark, but use caution. Remove the bullet or the shot from a round of ammunition and pour half of the powder into the tinder. Place a rag in the cartridge case and shoot it into the ground. The rag should burst into flame; it should then be placed in the tinder.

7. **A lens from a magnifying glass, binoculars or camera**. Any convex lens can produce a spark. Focus the sun's rays through the lens onto a small amount of good tinder. When it glows, blow on it gently.

8. **Emergency flares**. Shoot an emergency flare onto the ground to start a fire. Have carefully prepared tinder ready to put on the burning flare.

TINDER

Tinder is any material that will ignite from a small spark. It may be dead, dry grasses, bits of cotton, dry bark from the inside of cedar or birch trees, seed down from thistles, dried-out pine cones, dried moss, bits of dried bird's nest or gas-soaked rags. Prepare the tinder in a small pile the shape of a teepee, about 5 cm high. Put the shortest, driest pieces on the bottom.

You can also use a sliver of pitch or a strip of waxed fire starter. In extremely wet weather, the most available tinder is the tiny brittle branches from dead tree limbs. No larger than a pencil lead, they will burn even when damp. Ones from evergreen trees are especially good. Select ones that snap when broken off.

Note that tinder absorbs moisture readily from the atmosphere and may be least effective when you most urgently require it. Keep your tinder dry.

FUEL

In going from the tinder to the fuel stage in fire lighting, remember that large fuel materials require greater heat to ignite. Therefore, it is essential that some form of kindling be used to nurture the fire until it is hot enough to ignite larger fuel. A few suggestions for kindling are:

1. Dry, dead, evergreen twigs
2. Birch bark, shavings, wood chips or fine splinters of resinous wood
3. Feather sticks—dry sticks shaved on the sides into a fan shape
4. Gasoline or oil-impregnated wood

To maintain the fire, gather a good supply of fuel before you attempt to light the tinder. Different types of fuel are desirable for different circumstances. Use what is available, bearing in mind that all woods burn better when dry and that pitchy woods or wet woods smoke. Soft woods make the best kindling, and split branches burn faster than whole ones. The more finely the wood is split, the less smoky the fire will be. The denser the dry wood, the hotter the fire and usually the slower burning. Green wood will burn but requires a hot fire to get it started. If you have only green wood, split it fine and start with very small pieces.

OXYGEN
A fire requires oxygen. Ensure that the fire is well ventilated.

ADDITIONAL TIPS
1. Build your fire in a teepee shape around the tinder. After you get a blaze going, however, you may not wish to keep it teepee

shaped, since a teepee shape uses more wood than a fire in which the logs lie horizontally.

2. Start with a small fire and add to it as the flame increases. Do not add fuel too fast—allow the flame to grow gradually.

3. Blowing lightly on the burning wood increases the flame. Since fire climbs, always add new kindling above the flame.

4. Keep firewood dry under your shelter. Dry damp wood near the fire.

5. Always save some of the best kindling for the next fire.

6. Whenever possible, build a fire without using your matches. You will require matches to quickly light your signal fires or for other emergency uses.

7. To make a fire last overnight, place a layer of dry green logs over it. This banked fire will still be smouldering in the morning. It is easier to keep a fire going than to light one.

8. In anticipation of search planes, keep a supply of kindling and wood nearby so that a fire can quickly be set. Also helpful are some green or wet leaves, which, during the day, could quickly create a smoke signal to a search plane.

7 BUILDING A SHELTER

A shelter keeps you warm and dry and provides a much-needed boost to your morale. It will probably be built under difficult conditions and may be primitive, but it is better than nothing. Without shelter, precious body heat is lost. When properly constructed—insulated from the ground, protected from the wind and heated by a small fire—it will keep you dry and warm. The best shelter is one that includes all these features but, most important, will not require the use of too much energy to build.

You must use common sense and ingenuity when you are constructing a survival shelter. Use as much natural material as possible. Try to get into a forested area, since it can supply all the materials you'll need for heat, light and shelter.

LOCATION

Your first job is to find an area that can accommodate the shelter and a fire. Ideally, you want a spot that can easily be seen by rescuers, but it also has to be sheltered from the wind. Take into consideration the direction of the wind. In winter you don't want an icy wind blowing through the camp, so select a sheltered spot. In summer a light breeze may be welcome, since it helps drive away insects. Consider that you require a source of water. If the site is close to a stream, look for a high-water mark and remember that mountainous streams can rise as much as 6 or 7 m. Keep in mind also that running water can be noisy and may obliterate sounds of danger or the sound of a rescue plane. Choose a level campsite higher than the surrounding area so that there is good drainage. Do not camp near a game trail. Select a spot where the sun will reach the camp during some part of the day.

There is a variety of shelters that can be erected, and what you build must be based on four important factors: availability of materials, weather, location and your physical condition. Survey

the materials that you have with you—for example, a tarp and a knife—but be prepared to improvise and use what you see around you. Several recommended shelters are described here, and as with all aspects of survival, your imagination can greatly improve these basic designs.

NATURAL SHELTERS

Cave shelter

In the mountains or along the shores of rivers and lakes, caves or overhanging cliffs can provide shelter. Caves often require little work to be made livable—but don't forget that they may already be occupied. Smaller caves may be inhabited by mice or bats; a large one may house a bear family. Be observant and check for dung and footprints.

Caution should be exercised when you are investigating caves or overhanging cliffs. Caves usually have a wet floor, which makes footing hazardous. Loose rocks may be precariously lodged in the ceiling and may fall with the slightest disturbance. Never explore deep caves without first tying a string or fishing line at the mouth of the cave so that if you get lost inside, you can follow the string back out. If you use a cave for shelter, stay near the mouth, where the air is fresher and your fire will prevent animals from entering. Make sure that an overhanging cliff is of sound rock. Some strata are prone to breaking off and can be dangerous.

Fallen-tree shelter

Mountain rescue personnel often recommend the simple, under-the-log type of shelter. Find a log with a pit or shallow hole under it. Dig out and enlarge this natural pit. Use slabs of bark and boughs to line the walls and floor. Keep your living area small.

Near the ocean, you can build a driftwood frame that can be covered with plastic, seaweed or coniferous branches. Note: Make sure that the shelter is built above the high-tide mark or you may awaken with water rising inside the shelter.

Rock shelter

Along rocky sea coasts and above the treeline, rock shelters are often the only type you will be able to build. Rock cairns constructed as blinds for waterfowl hunters are ideal. These are simple rock constructions in the shape of a large U with the opening in the leeward side, where a fire is built. Cracks can be filled with seaweed. This is not an ideal shelter, but anything that provides protection will be welcome.

Above the timberline, it may be difficult to find a suitable shelter, but a bluff on the leeward side of the wind can be used to advantage. If the bluff overhangs the site and has a lot of loose rock, it may be too dangerous to consider for a shelter. In an area with large, loose rocks, two wings can be built—one on each side to cut down on the eddying wind currents. Having two wings will protect your shelter, and the heat from your fire will reflect from the vertical wall, making it comfortable and warm. Moving large rocks consumes a great deal of energy, however, so pace yourself. Smoke in a shelter is a problem, but a little smoke is less unpleasant than a night without a fire.

THE LEAN-TO

When constructing a lean-to, find two trees 2 or 3 m apart with fairly level, firm ground between them. The distance between the trees will be the length of the opening of the lean-to, although it is possible to incorporate variations. The number of people requiring shelter should determine the size of the lean-to. When constructed for one, it should be made long enough for you to sleep across the mouth of the shelter. For more than one, it should be designed for all to sleep lengthwise. You may support one or both ends of the ridge pole with a pole bipod or tripod instead of using standing trees, meaning that you have a wider choice of sites. Remember that the steeper the slope angle of the roof, the better it will shed precipitation and reflect heat from the fire. A 45-degree slope angle is considered a suitable compromise between available interior space and rain-shedding effectiveness.

After the framework has been constructed, proceed with the covering. Spruce boughs make an excellent natural covering, although the branches of any coniferous and of many deciduous trees will do. They are placed on the lean-to in the same manner as shingles on a roof, the first row at the bottom. The brush ends of the boughs are placed down, overlapping the butt ends of the previous row. This method of thatching ensures that rain will be

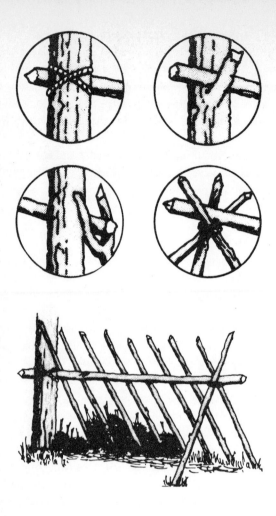

readily shed. Continue to lay rows of boughs in this fashion until the top of the lean-to is covered. Then repeat the thatching procedure until the entire roof is covered to a depth of at least 15 cm. The triangular sides are filled in with large boughs set butt-end up, as in thatching. The lean-to frame can also be covered with bark, rushes, split-wood planks, canvas or your heat-reflective space blanket.

TARP SHELTER

A tarp, a sheet of plastic, an emergency space blanket, a piece of parachute or garbage bags can all be used for shelter. One method
is to use rope from your survival kit, attach it between two trees and drape your covering over the rope. Fasten it to the ground by driving sticks through it or piling rocks or sand on it.

Shelters from Tarps

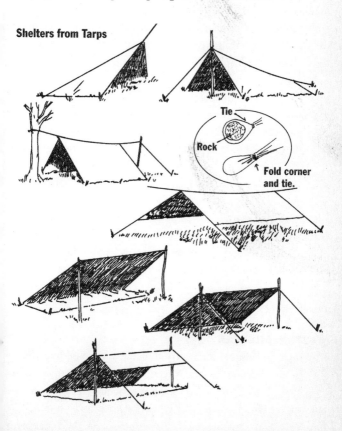

WIGWAM

In wooded areas, wigwams can provide suitable shelter for as many as 10 people. The first step is to select three main poles approximately 3 m long and 7 cm thick. Tie these poles in an upright position with the tied ends up. Spread them so that the distance from the ground to the top of the tripod, where the poles are secured, is approximately 2 m measured vertically. To provide support for the cone of your wigwam, select several side poles, 5 cm thick and the same length as the three main poles.

To hold the side and main poles in position, place short poles on the ground between the side and main poles. Cover the frame with canvas or any other suitable material. Tie any separate pieces of this covering together. Leave a portion of the covering for an entrance downwind. When boughs or branches are your only source of covering, use more side poles to provide a closer meshed frame on which to weave. In winter, bank the lower edge of the completed wigwam with snow to prevent a draught.

To build a bed, gather evergreen boughs (spruce work well). Trim the ends off each branch to about 20 to 30 cm in length. Set the ends aside and spread the branches flat in your bed area to a thickness of approximately 15 cm. Stick the ends at slight angles between the boughs so that they cover the branches. Note: Do not use moss, since it soaks up water.

To heat your wigwam, build a small fire directly in the centre, after you have made a small draught channel under the wall and a small hole in the top. Although not all the smoke will escape, when mosquitoes, black flies and other insects are numerous, a little smoke will not matter.

WINTER SHELTER

Although you should always try to get to the timberline, there may be times when you are forced to make camp on an open alpine meadow. Try to look on snow as a friend. It is readily available material from which many types of shelter can be built.

The snow cave

In both treeless and forested terrain, the snow cave is a relatively good shelter. The first step is to select a deep snowdrift of about 2 m high and close to 4 m wide. A riverbed, ravine, high bank or overhang usually proves the best spot. Avoid newly fallen powder snow, avalanche paths or frozen snow that is too heavily packed. Take care when you select the entrance. The wind should not blow into the cave or drifting snow will block the entrance.

Next burrow a small tunnel directly into the side of the drift for about 60 cm. From the end of the tunnel, dig out a chamber. If you don't have a shovel, a snowshoe will work. The roof should be about 50 cm thick. It is best to dig to the right and left so that the chamber is at a right angle to the tunnel entrance. If you dig along the axis of the tunnel, you may run into old snow, which is more difficult to dig than new snow. To help speed up the work, a second entrance can be made. This can be sealed when the cave is completed.

A quicker method of construction, because it permits more people to work, is to dig into the bank along the complete length of the cave to the depth you need. Afterwards, build a snow wall along the outside, leaving only a narrow gap for the entrance.

Regardless of the size of your snow cave, the following building principles should be followed. The tunnel entrance should lead into the lowest level of the chamber—that is, to the bottom of the pit, where cooking is done and equipment is stored. Because cold air is heavy and does not rise, outside air coming into the cave will not spread if it comes in at the lowest level. Keep the entrance small. When not in use, the entrance should be blocked, or partially covered, with a snow block. Note: When the entrance is blocked, the cave is airtight. Have a shovel inside with you in case you need to dig yourself out.

The sleeping benches should be higher than the highest point of the tunnel entrance to avoid unnecessary draughts—approximately 45 cm is ideal. The only warm air lost is that

which is allowed to escape through the ventilation shaft in the roof.

The roof of the cave should be high enough to provide comfortable sitting space. The roof must be arched so that it will be strong and so that the drops of water on the inside, caused by melting, will not drop straight down on the floor but will follow the curved sides, glazing over the walls when refrozen.

There should be at least two ventilators, one in the roof and one in the door. If these ventilators are allowed to close, you may become asphyxiated, especially when you are cooking. Beware of carbon monoxide fumes. A burning candle warns of oxygen deficiency.

The quinzhee

An Inuit quinzhee is an excellent shelter in wet snow, though it can be built in powder as well. Choose a wind-sheltered site, measure a circle 2 m in diameter and pile snow to about the same height. After packing the outside layer of snow well, allow it to harden for an hour or so. (Powder snow will take longer.) When it is safe to walk on, you can carve out the interior of the mound. Make the entrance crawl height, and in the main area you'll want adequate head space when you kneel. The roof should be about 20 cm thick and the walls approximately 45 cm thick. Carve out a sleeping bench and punch out several holes for ventilation.

Snow walls

On alpine meadows, when no other shelter is available, a snow wall can be built. To make this shelter, cut snow blocks from compact snow and use them to build a semicircular wall to a height of approximately 1 m. Bank the wall with loose snow on the windward side to provide a windbreak to sleep behind.

The snow hole

Faced with the necessity of providing yourself with immediate, quick shelter, dig a snow hole. Burrow into a snowdrift or dig a trench in the snow. Use fir boughs for insulation if available. Make a roof of any handy material, boughs, branches or snow blocks supported on skis or snowshoes. To provide the warmest spot for yourself, build a bench that is higher than the opening. This is a temporary shelter and should be replaced as soon as possible.

8 WATER

Water is more necessary for survival than food. Adults require approximately 2 L a day; anything less leads to dehydration. Keep in mind that most people who are lost are found within 72 hours, and as long as you have water, you can survive on your body fat. When in the backcountry, don't wait until you are out of water before accumulating more. Water is essential.

WATER WARNING

Do not drink salt water. It aggravates your thirst and may cause further loss of body fluids through diarrhea and vomiting.

It is no longer safe to drink water directly from streams in British Columbia. *Giardia* is a single-cell organism that is transmitted through animal and human waste. Untreated water from lakes, streams or ponds infected with it causes giardiasis, commonly called beaver fever. It may be several weeks before symptoms similar to that of a bad stomach flu appear. If you suspect you have beaver fever see your doctor.

IF YOU ARE SHORT OF WATER

It is better to conserve what water you have in your body by reducing water loss in every way possible.

1. Avoid overexertion.
2. Never drink alcohol.
3. Keep cool. Stay in the shade.
4. Limit the amount of food you eat and restrict it to carbohydrates, such as starches and sugars, as much as possible. It takes significantly more water to digest protein.

FINDING WATER IN SUMMER

This province is blessed with an abundance of water.

1. Fast-running streams are common in mountainous regions. Don't believe the theory that because it is running water (even over rock beds), it is safe to drink. But streams or small waterfalls are excellent places to gather water, which you then must treat (see section entitled "Purification of Water" on page 46).

2. Lakes, ponds, sloughs, swamps and muskeg areas all provide water that can be treated for drinking.

3. In muskeg areas where the vegetation is in mounds of varying heights, you may find small pools of water around the base of a mound.

4. In rocky mountain areas, check crevices for trapped water.

5. Look in valley bottoms and, if there are no streams, dig in patches of green, damp vegetation.

6. If there is no surface water, you can also dig in gullies and dry streambeds.

7. Make containers to collect rainwater. Line a hollow tree trunk with a garbage bag or simply use a piece of bark to collect rainwater.

8. In arid conditions, dig a pit about 50 cm deep and place a pot or cup on the bottom. Cover the top of the pit with plastic held in place by rocks or sand. Place a rock on top of the plastic directly above the container. The condensation that collects on the plastic will accumulate below the rock and drip down into the container.

9. If you have a de-salter kit, sea water can be used.

10. On the shoreline well above high-tide mark, dig deep and the seepage can be treated to drink.

11. Watch animals, birds and insects to find water sources. Grazing animals and grain-eating birds are seldom far from water. (Water birds and birds of prey are not good indicators, since they do not drink frequently.)

12. Dew from plants—especially large-leafed ones—can be stripped.

FINDING WATER IN WINTER

1. Use ice from lakes or streams to obtain water.
2. Ice is a better source of water than snow. It takes twice as much heat to obtain moisture from snow than from ice. You must have your fire, a stove, fuel and a pot to melt the ice.
3. After ensuring that the ice is safe to walk on, break the ice with a pointed instrument, make light taps to start a crack and then give one sharp tap to break off a chunk. On a large lake or stream surface, cut along an existing crack to avoid getting only splinters and spray.
4. Hard-packed snow yields more water than fluffy snow. To melt snow, put small amounts in a pot and compress it or the bottom of the pot will burn. If you have some water, put it in the pot first and then add snow gradually to keep the pot from burning.
5. Do not eat ice or snow. Your body gives up heat to melt the ice or snow. Because it is cold, it tends to dehydrate the body. If heat is not available, melt small quantities of snow by squeezing and breathing on it and drinking the water droplets.
6. Snow that has been on sea ice for some time usually contains salt.
7. Salt-free ice may be found where the ice has aged. This ice is found in areas that the sun seldom reaches or perhaps along the top of ridges where salt has leached out. Old ice is bluish with a crystalline structure, as opposed to salty ice, which is grey and opaque. Be cautious, however, as old ice may have been sprayed by sea water.

PURIFICATION OF WATER

All water must be treated.

1. Boil water 10 minutes. In the mountains, boil it an additional minute for each 300 m of elevation.
2. There are some excellent filtering systems. They come in the

form of a small cup or plastic bottle with a filter attached and fit easily into your day pack or pocket. There may be a slight taste to this water, but germs have been killed. Note that very cold water filters slowly.

3. There are water purification tablets that use either iodine or chlorine to kill germs. It has not been proven that they will kill *Giardia*. Be sure to check the expiry dates on these tablets.

4. Water can be treated with iodine drops. Add 5 drops to a litre of clear water and 10 drops to a litre of cloudy water. Allow it to sit 30 minutes before drinking.

5. The flavour of safe but unpalatable water is improved by adding charcoal from the fire and allowing it to sit overnight.

KEEPING WATER UNPOLLUTED

Although there is no perfect means of disposing of waste in the backcountry, it is important to be as careful as possible. Improper disposal of human waste is a serious health threat.

When camping, never urinate or defecate directly into water or near a water source. Dig a hole 10 to 15 cm deep and, after each use, spread a layer of light soil in the hole. This "cat hole" should be at least 100 m from any water source. Burn or pack out all toilet paper. As with garbage, the rule of thumb is—if you pack it in, pack it out.

9 FOOD

Food is not an immediate requirement for survival. A healthy person with plenty of water can live several weeks without food. In cold weather or during periods of strenuous activity, however, food is required to maintain your body temperature and keep up your energy level. A balanced diet is always important—even when in the backcountry vary what you are eating as much as possible.

FINDING FOOD

It is important to ration your emergency food supply and attempt to find local foods. A survival guide will assist you in identifying edible plants and with fishing and hunting skills.

1. All fur-bearing animals are edible, and animal food gives you the most food value per kilogram.
2. All grass seeds are edible.
3. In general, there is more food value in roots and tubers than in greens, but remember that greens provide important vitamins C and A.
4. Keep an open mind about eating strange foods. Learn to overcome your prejudices—foods that are unusual to you are often part of the regular diet of others.
5. Do not eat shellfish from beds where large quantities of them are already dead.
6. During summer months, mussels and clams rapidly assimilate certain toxins present in the water, and eating them can result in a paralytic poisoning. Note: Avoid eating mussels and clams from April through October. At other times of the year, they can be found in large quantities clinging to rocks along the beach at low tide and can be steamed and eaten.
7. Sea urchins, which look like animated purple or green

pincushions, are edible. Break them open; the red or yellow egg masses (gonads) can be eaten raw.

8. Snails and limpets creeping on rocks are often more plentiful than other sea life. Cook by boiling for 10 minutes, but eat in small amounts to make sure that you don't have an allergic reaction to them. (Avoid snails with brightly coloured shells; they may be poisonous.)

9. All birds are edible. Pluck them instead of skinning them because most of their fat is in the skin.

10. Although not plentiful in British Columbia, snakes and lizards are edible. Remove the head, entrails and skin, and they are ready for the pot. There are rattlesnakes in some areas, but they are considered too dangerous to be a good source of food.

11. The larvae or grubs of many insects are edible and nourishing. Grubs are found in rotten logs, in the ground and under the bark of dead trees. They should be boiled or fried but can be eaten raw. To eat grasshoppers, remove the wings, legs and head; cook the body, since it may contain harmful parasites. Don't eat caterpillars—many are poisonous.

12. The inner bark of many trees is edible—for example, poplars (including cottonwoods and aspens), willows, alders and some conifers, such as pines, hemlocks and spruces (not cedars or yews). After removing the outer bark, strip or scrape the inner bark from the trunk and eat it fresh or cooked. It can also be dried. It is thickest and most palatable when newly formed in spring. At this time of the year in mountainous country it may be the only reliable source of solid plant food.

13. Teas can be made from spruce and fir needles and the leaves of Labrador tea, a shrub of the heather family.

14. There is a great variety of blue, black, red and white berries to be found in British Columbia. It is important to identify the species before you eat them. In general, do not eat berries that taste bad.

15. Don't eat the seed kernels of wild cherries; they are poisonous.

16. Avoid plants with orange, yellow, red, dark or soapy-tasting sap or sap that rapidly turns black on exposure to the air.

17. Avoid plants resembling beans, cucumbers, melons or parsnips. Some are extremely poisonous.

18. Although many seaweeds are edible, they are difficult to digest. Avoid Desmarestia, which is poisonous. It is brownish to olive-green and grows in a single axis with cylindrical leaves. It is found on rocks below the low-tide mark.

PREPARING FOOD

1. Boiling is the best way to cook food, since it preserves juices. You should then drink the juices.

2. Another method is to wrap food, such as fish or root vegetables, in leaves or seaweed and bury it in a preheated rock-lined pit from which the fire has been removed. Make sure that you do not use leaves from poisonous plants. Cover the wrapped food with more leaves and a layer of dirt. Don't disturb for several hours.

3. To roast meat, skewer it and rotate it above the fire. A slow roast cooks meat best; the spit should be to one side of the flames with a container beside the fire to catch fat for basting.

4. You can build a grate out of green branches and grill food above hot embers.

5. It is important to cook food well, since the heat kills germs and harmful parasites. Cooking may also make the food more digestible.

OTHER TIPS

• Always test a new plant food for edibility. Chew a teaspoonful of it well and hold it in your mouth for five minutes. If there is no burning, soapy, nauseating or bitter taste, swallow it and wait eight hours. If you suffer no ill effects, repeat with a mouthful and wait another eight hours. If there are no adverse effects, go ahead and eat the food.

- The human body reacts quickly to unaccustomed plant foods. Even when food is prepared properly, it may give you a stomach ache. Rely on fish, animal meat and fruits that you know will provide energy. Ration your food supply that you carried with you.
- To conserve energy, minimize muscle activity. Look for energy-efficient ways to do chores. Try to control shivering, since it uses up energy.
- To overcome discomfort from hunger and acid buildup, use antacid tablets from your first-aid kit.

SOME EDIBLE PLANTS TO KNOW

Kinnikinnick (Bearberry)

This perennial is low growing and spreads in mats because of its long, freely rooting shoots. Its evergreen leaves are thick, tough, tapered at the base and shiny dark green on top. The leaves, about 25 mm long, are oval and alternate. The clustered flowers are waxy, urn shaped and white to pinkish. They mature into round, bright red berries, about 1 cm across. Berries, which are an excellent source of carbohydrates, are ripe from late summer until spring. Although they can be eaten raw, they are mealy and seedy. They can also be fried or added to soups and stews.

Kinnikinnick

Cattail

Cattail

This easily identified plant grows in wet areas and is an excellent source of starch and sugar. Pull, dig or cut the rhizome and peel it. The roots can be eaten raw or boiled. They taste like potato after they have been boiled for 30 minutes. You can also mash the fresh-peeled roots and soak them in a container of water, stirring occasionally to loosen the starch from the fibres. When the water is cloudy, allow it to stand overnight so that the starch will settle on the bottom. Then pour off the excess water and scoop out the thick, sticky dough for roasting, baking or boiling.

In spring the green shoots, which grow from the root, can be cut, peeled and boiled about 15 minutes and eaten. Be cautious about gathering shoots if the water the cattail grows in is contaminated. In addition, the young, greenish flower spikes can be boiled and eaten much like corn on the cob. Later in the season, the pollen from the upper spikes can be eaten and is high in protein.

Wild rose

There is a variety of species of wild roses. Most are thorned, and their branched stems grow from 1 to 3 m in height. Leaves are

Wild Rose

dark green, compound and toothed. The five-petalled blossoms are pale to deep pink and are singular or clustered on the young branches. Late in summer, the fruit, known as rose hips, begins to swell and darken. By autumn, the rose hips become orange-to-red tufted berry-like fruits, which are easily recognized and often cling to the shrubs all winter.

Rose hips are best when brightly coloured. Pare off the tuft at the ends of the hips, cut them in half and remove seeds. They can be eaten raw, cooked like any fresh fruit, boiled down to a syrup, partially dried to be eaten like raisins or thoroughly dried and crushed into a powder to be used in soups and teas. Strain off the seeds, since they can irritate your throat and digestive tract. Rose petals and young, tender shoots are also edible.

Wild berries

Blueberries, blackberries, gooseberries, wild strawberries, salmonberries, thimbleberries and serviceberries are some of the many varieties that grow in the province. Many are easily recognizable because they resemble the cultivated varieties. Some of them are more tasty than their garden counterpart. Wild raspberries, for example, although smaller and rounder, are superior in flavour to cultivated raspberries. Serviceberries, the B.C. species of saskatoon berries, are often sweet and juicy. The berries resemble large, tufted blueberries and are ripe early to mid-summer. Most berries are rich in vitamin C; don't overlook them as a food source.

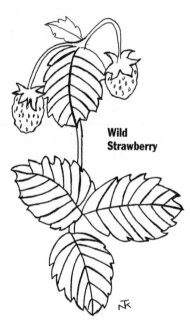

Wild Strawberry

Fireweed

This tall herb—often up to 2 m high—has showy, four-petalled flowers that grow in elongated clusters and are reddish-purple. Fireweed grows in disturbed soil such as burns and logged areas and is abundant in British Columbia.

The young shoots, leaves and budded flower stalks are rich in vitamin C and can be eaten raw or cooked like spinach. Like many greens, though, they have laxative properties. Mature leaves can be dried for tea. The seed fluff can be used for tinder.

Fireweed

Pine trees

Pines such as lodgepole, ponderosa and whitebark have clusters of needle-like leaves and cones, which vary in size depending on the species. For example, the lodgepole pine has egg-shaped

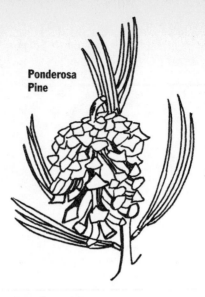

Ponderosa Pine

cones about 3 cm long, whereas the ponderosa has cones 8 to 16 cm long. Squirrels often collect and cache seeds from these trees.

The inner bark and cambium of pines is a well-known wild edible. It can be eaten raw or cooked; it can also be dried for later use. The green needles of the pines, an excellent source of vitamin C, can be used for tea. Note: This tea should never be drunk by pregnant women. The seeds are edible, but except for whitebark, which has seeds the size of peanuts, most are too small to be of any consequence.

Wapato arrowhead

The bright green leaves of this aquatic or semi-aquatic plant are often gracefully shaped like a broadhead arrow tip. The single flower stalk bears several three-petalled waxy white flowers near its tip. Blooms appear in summer and may last until nearly autumn, at which time they mature to rounded capsules. The fibrous roots spread through mud from the leaf stalks, and in the

**Wapato
Arrowhead**

fall, small tubers mature on the roots. These are edible and can be harvested by wading into the cold water, feeling with your hands and feet and kicking or pulling up the tubers, which float to the surface. Another approach is to fashion a rake and, from the shore, rake through the top 15 cm of mud, breaking the tubers free so that they float up to be gathered. Cook tubers until soft. They taste similar to sweet potatoes.

Bog cranberry

Found in bogs and marshes, this cranberry usually grows with sphagnum or peat moss. It is a creeping, vine-like evergreen shrub with tiny, glossy leaves that have spotted, lighter undersides. The flowers range from pink to red with reflexed petals

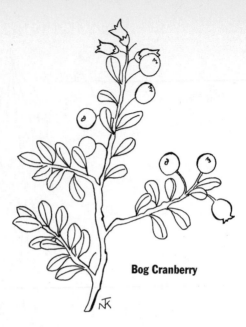

Bog Cranberry

and grow at the ends of thin stems. They mature to berries—similar to commercial cranberries but smaller—which become bright red in late autumn.

The ripe berries, which have a tendency to cling to the vine all winter, can be harvested anytime but are best in the fall after a frost. They are tart when eaten raw but can be cooked and sugar can be added. They taste similar to the supermarket variety.

Mountain cranberry

This evergreen sub-shrub with tufted branches grows to 15 cm tall. The leaves are elliptic and leathery and have scattered black glands on the underleaf; they resemble boxwood. The small flowers are white or pink and the berries, which are bright red, remain on the vines until the following spring.

Like bog cranberries, the berries are tart but edible and improve with cooking. Mix with sugar or other berries to sweeten.

Dandelion

The dandelion is characterized by a long taproot and by a rosette of green, toothed leaves spreading from the root crown. The reddish-brown stem is hollow and supports first a conical, green tufted bud and then a round, bright yellow flower. Finally, there appears a spherical silver-grey and fluffy seed head. The sap, or latex, of the weed is milky and bitter.

The root, somewhat bitter, can be dug at any time and boiled like carrots. In spring, the young leaves can be used as salad greens or can be cooked as an herb to add to other dishes. The leaves have a high nutritional value. If either the root or the leaves are too bitter, change the cooking water and boil again.

Dandelion

Oregon grape

Found growing beneath trees and dry hillside thickets, the holly-like, dark green leaves of this evergreen shrub are thick and smooth surfaced. In spring, yellow flowers form dense clusters and the dark blue berries have a white, waxy coating. The berries, which are very tart, are best stewed with sugar or with other berries to sweeten them. They are a good source of vitamin C but should not be consumed in large quantities or as a regular part of your diet, since they contain one potentially toxic ingredient.

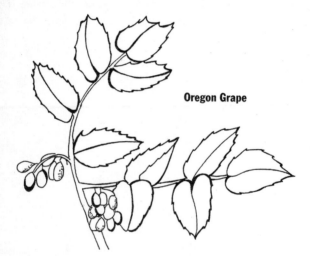

Oregon Grape

Mountain sorrel

Growing at higher altitudes, often in wet, rocky terrain, mountain sorrel has an erect stem, kidney-shaped leaves and small red or green flowers that grow in clusters. The leaves and stems can be eaten raw or cooked. Mountain sorrel can be harvested in spring, summer and often into fall and is a good source of vitamin C. This rhubarb-like plant (sometimes called scurvy grass) should be eaten in small quantities, however, because it contains oxalic acid and can cause stomach upset if eaten in excess.

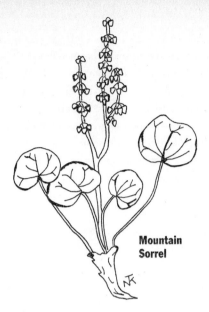

Mountain Sorrel

Maple

There are three species of maple in British Columbia. Vine maple is slender and multi-stemmed; Rocky Mountain maple is a small, bushy tree; and broad-leaved maple grows into a large spreading tree up to 30 m tall. The leaves of the first two are relatively small and turn red in fall; broad-leaved maples turn golden yellow in fall. At this time the seeds, each with a wing, mature and begin to drop, attached in pairs.

The seeds are edible raw or roasted. The inner bark can be stripped and pounded for flour. In spring, sap can be obtained by drilling into the tree. The sweet, thin sap is both nutritious and moisture giving.

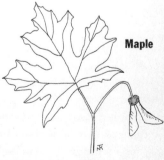

Maple

Crowberry

Low, matted and spreading, this evergreen shrub grows in sub-alpine, alpine and muskeg areas. It has needle-like linear leaves resembling the twigs of a small fir tree. Flowers are small, solitary and white. The berries grow along the stem singly or in small clusters and are purplish to black. They have large, hard seeds.

The juicy berries can be eaten raw or stored. They have a mildly medicinal flavour, which some people dislike. In the Arctic, where they are called blackberries, they are an important fruit, since they may be found year-round.

Crowberry

Salal

Plentiful in coastal British Columbia, this wiry shrub may be creeping or grow to a height of about 2.5 m, often in dense patches. An evergreen, it has leathery, ovate leaves with pointed

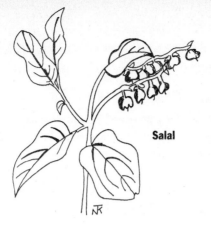

Salal

tips. Flowers grow in one-sided clusters and are urn shaped and white to pinkish. The berries are plump, hairy and dark blue to blackish.

The berries from healthy bushes are flavourful and juicy. In some cases, though, they may be mealy or grainy. Nonetheless, salal is an excellent source of food. The berries can be eaten raw or cooked and can also be dried.

Labrador tea

This evergreen, aromatic shrub may grow as high as 200 cm in dense patches in peat bogs, muskegs and wet mountain meadows. Leaves grow near the tops of the plant, are oblong and have dense, rust-coloured hairs underneath. Flowers are white or creamy in terminal, umbrella-shaped clusters.

Use the leaves, which are fragrant when crushed, for tea. The pungent taste may be reduced by

Labrador Tea

using two changes of boiling water. Make the tea weak, since it is said to have narcotic properties. Beware—do not confuse this plant with swamp laurel, which is toxic. It has pink flowers and does not have the fuzzy under-leaf.

Wild onion

Leaves are tubular, narrow and generally shorter than the flower stem. The flowers, white to pink, grow at the end of the stalk and often appear after the grass-like leaves have died down.

The bulbs of this perennial have a characteristic onion odour and can be boiled to lessen the strong taste. Wild onion is excellent for flavouring soups and stews.

Wild Onion

Common plantain

As well known as dandelion, plantain has smooth-edged, broadly elliptical leaves that may grow to 25 cm in length. Flowers are small, green and inconspicuous and grow at the top

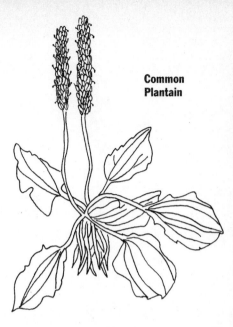

Common Plantain

of a leafless stem. Seed capsules are egg shaped and produce 6 to 30 seeds that are about 1 mm long and sticky when wet.

The leaves can be eaten raw in salads or cooked to be eaten like spinach or as a potherb. Young growth is best, but sugar or honey can be added to mature leaves to improve the taste. Plantain tea can be made by boiling two large handfuls in 1 L of water for 30 minutes. It is rich in vitamins A and C.

Giant knotweed

Named for its thickened joints, which resemble knots, this perennial may grow to a height of 2.5 cm; stems are reddish-brown, wand-like and hollow. Knotweed leaves are large—to 20 cm in length—and oval shaped. Whitish-green flowers grow in clusters in the leaf axils.

The young underground rhizomes can be boiled or roasted; the young shoots can be boiled 3 to 5 minutes, and the leaves can be used as salad greens. Do not eat large quantities, since some species can cause hypersensitivity to light.

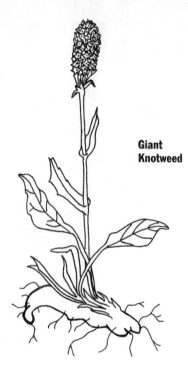

Giant Knotweed

POISONOUS PLANTS

Described here are a few of the poisonous plants that are found in British Columbia. Use common sense; when in doubt, don't sample a wild plant.

Mushrooms

There are many types of fungi; many are edible, but some are poisonous. Since it is so difficult to distinguish between those that are safe to eat and those that may cause an upset stomach or kill you, don't eat wild mushrooms.

Water hemlock

This herbaceous perennial has been called the most poisonous plant in North America. Found in swampy, wet areas, it is common in British Columbia and grows to a height of 2 m. The root is usually hollow and has cross-portions. It smells like a parsnip. The small white flowers can be confused with those of other plants, such as the cow parsnip or water parsnip. Do not eat any part of the plant or plants that are similar in description.

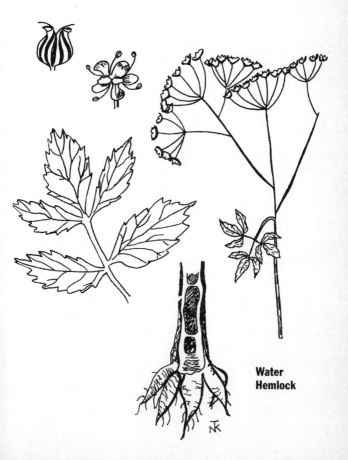

Water
Hemlock

Baneberry

Often growing up to 1 m high, the baneberry produces small white flowers followed by clusters of glossy white or red spherical berries. Berries and rootstalk are highly poisonous.

Baneberry

10 HUNTING AND FISHING

Should you be lost in the backcountry, there is a good probability that you will be rescued within a few days. There may be occasions, however, when this time stretches to the point that your survival depends on hunting animals and fishing. Unless you are skilled, this task will not be easy. If you are going to spend a lot of time in the wilderness, take courses to prepare for these occasions. Training and experience are invaluable for hunting and fishing.

HUNTING

In today's environmentally conscious atmosphere, hunting and snaring are seasonally controlled. Under normal conditions a licence is required for trapping and hunting in British Columbia; some designated government employees are authorized to carry firearms. If it is a matter of life and death, however, you must look after yourself. The advice given here is for authentic survival situations only.

Before you can catch animals, you must learn to read the signs that alert you to their presence. There is little use in setting a rabbit snare if there is no sign of the animal in the area. The following general rules should assist you:

1. **Remember that whenever you leave camp,** you must orient yourself to your surroundings and leave signs that you can follow back to camp.
2. **Move quietly and slowly,** stop frequently, look in all directions and listen.
3. **Hunt upwind or crosswind** whenever possible.
4. **Blend with the terrain features** as much as possible; for example, do not stand against the skyline or break from cover without thorough observation.

5. **Keep alert**—game can frequently startle you or catch you off guard.

6. **Be observant.** Animal movement and feeding are weather-dependent. For example, after a storm, animals will be out feeding. In general, large animals feed during the day; small animals eat at night.

7. **When you see an animal,** remain still and move only when it feeds. Should you have a weapon, make the opportunity count.

8. **Trails can provide good information.** Beaten down through heavy usage, they may show where the animals travel between their watering and feeding locales and their habitats. If recently used, trails are excellent places for setting snares.

9. **Tracks provide a wealth of information,** such as the type and size of animal, the direction taken, the age of tracks and

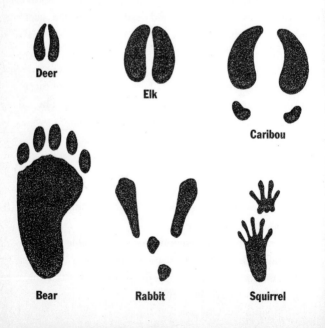

Deer

Elk

Caribou

Bear

Rabbit

Squirrel

whether the animal is frightened. The height of where the brush is broken indicates its size. The direction is determined by the way the branches are broken. Tracks are easiest to read on wet ground or in the snow. The clearer the track is, the more recently it has been made. In the morning, if the dew has been disturbed or a spider web broken, it is a sign that an animal has walked there recently. When tracks are farther apart, the animal is running.

10. **The size and quantity of droppings are among the best indications of what animal has passed.** Fresh droppings will be smelly and wet. A large amount of bird droppings may indicate a favourite roosting spot for birds.

11. **Feeding grounds, water holes and mineral licks are good locations for hunting in early morning or evening.** Freshly dug earth indicates that an animal has been in search of insects, small rodents or tubers. Trails leading to these sites may be suitable places for snares or traps.

12. **Dens, holes and food stores are found by following tracks and checking for droppings.** These are good spots for setting snares.

13. **Slow-moving animals, such as a porcupine, can be killed with a heavy stick.**

14. **Most small animals, such as squirrels and rabbits, are easily skinned.** For example, a rabbit is skinned by making an opening across the centre of the back and pulling the skin in opposite directions. Cut off the feet and head and remove the insides.

Snaring

To be used only in survival situations, snares will work for you day and night. Using rope, twine or wire, make a noose to catch a small animal by the neck or larger game by the legs. (Keep in mind that you will probably have to kill an animal caught in a leg snare.) Scout your immediate area to learn its game potential and set snares as soon as possible. Remember to establish a baseline or checkpoints so that you can find your way back to camp.

Snaring rabbits

There are several species of rabbits in British Columbia; in woodlands, they frequent heavy thickets. Snares should be set on their runways, preferably where the width of the trail is restricted by natural or human-made obstacles.

Close-up of the loop. Wires should be twisted together.

Sticks may be inserted into the ground to guide the rabbit into the snare.

12 cm

8 cm

Common Rabbit Snare (using wire)

Snaring squirrels

Squirrel caches are found in tree cavities, nests or holes in the ground. Don't bother checking a cache as a food source, since it will consist mainly of pine and spruce cones and some mushrooms. The leaning pole snare is a simple and effective method of catching squirrels. It should be used near their food caches or nests. Three or more snares to a pole are desirable, since squirrels are fond of the company of other squirrels.

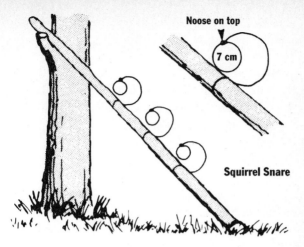

Noose on top

7 cm

Squirrel Snare

Snaring larger animals

Snares set in well-worn trails may save tedious hours of walking or waiting. A snare of cable or heavy wire 60 cm in diameter and suspended approximately 45 cm above the ground should produce good results. If the snare is well anchored, the animal will probably kill itself in a short time. Remember that killing an

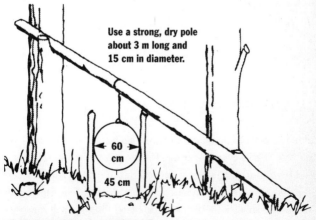

Use a strong, dry pole about 3 m long and 15 cm in diameter.

60 cm

45 cm

A Method of Snaring Antlered Game

animal is only the first step—it is a lot of work to skin and prepare a large animal.

FISHING

Since fish are a valuable food source and small fish are abundant, it is logical to turn to fishing in a survival situation. Although angling may be the most enjoyable method of fishing, there are other effective methods.

Set lines

This is an easy method of fishing that does not require the presence of the fisher. Set a line with a baited hook from a tree branch that will bend when you get a bite. This method works well at night. For bait consider insects, worms or parts of fish (eyes, fins, head or strips of belly). It's a good idea to check the stomach of the first fish caught to discover what it has eaten.

Netting

A gill net is most effective in still water—a lake near the inlet or outlet, or the backwater in a large stream. In a survival situation,

Gill Net Set for Summer Use

don't hesitate to block the stream. Nets can be constructed using cord, string or even tree roots. Use floats on top and weights on the bottom to keep the net vertical in the water. When ice is on the lake, the fish are inclined to stay deeper. The smaller the mesh, the smaller the fish you can catch, but a small mesh will still entangle a large fish. A mesh of 6 cm is a good standard.

Although making a net is time-consuming, it may be worthwhile, since all marine life is edible.

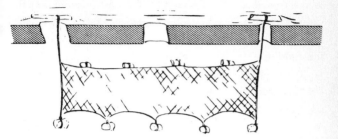

Gill Net Set for Winter Use

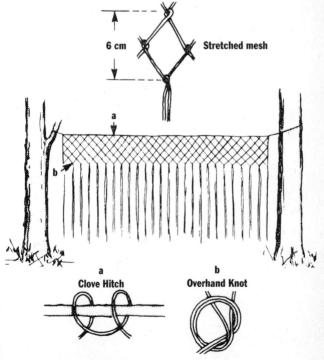

6 cm — Stretched mesh

a — Clove Hitch

b — Overhand Knot

Construction of a Gill Net

Snaring fish

The snare consists of a loop of wire attached to a long pole. The loop is passed over the fish's head and the fish is jerked from the water. This works best in shallow water when fish are spawning.

Ice fishing

If the ice is safe to walk on, use a hatchet or axe to cut a hole in the ice. Try to fish in a water depth of 1.5 to 2.5 m, since the fish can be brought up quickly and so have less chance to break your line or tear out the hook. Keep the bait (spinners or wobblers) moving to attract fish. Jigging is another technique—use a short stick, a fish line and a shiny object near the hook to attract fish. Tip-up fishing allows you to get away from the cold ice. Set up one stick across the ice hole and tie another stick across it with a fish hook and bait in the water. When this stick tips up, you have a fish.

11 KNOTS

Your life may depend on your ability to properly tie knots. A poorly constructed snare, a lost gill net and a tarp that blows away in the night are a few of the problems you may avoid if you familiarize yourself with the various types of knots. The important ones are illustrated:

Thumb Knot
Stops unravelling of the rope.

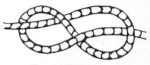

Figure of Eight
Prevents the rope from being pulled through the pulley.

Reef Knot
For joining two ropes of equal diameter.

Sheet Bend
For joining two ropes of unequal diameter.

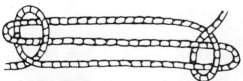

Sheep Shank
For shortening a rope that is tied at both ends.

Hawser Bend
For tying two large
ropes together.

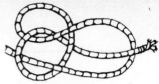

Bowline
For making a non-slip
loop in the end of a rope.

Running Bowline
For making a running
loop in the end of a rope.

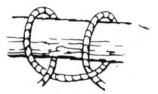

Clove Hitch
Mooring knot.

Timber Hitch
For hauling or
towing lumber.

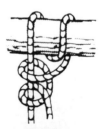

Round Hitch
Two half hitches.
Mooring knot.

12 <u>TRAVEL</u>

The decision to move in the wilderness is a serious one. Once you are lost or injured, you must set up camp, build a fire and stay close to the camp in hope of a rescue. Most rescues are made when the hiker stays in one place. Wandering aimlessly wastes energy and complicates the situation for yourself and those looking for you.

In making the decision to move, you must consider your mental and physical condition, the weather, distances, terrain, and your supply of food, water and fuel. Examples of good reasons to move are lack of food and water or a local danger, such as a bear in the area. There are five basic requirements for travel; if any of them cannot be met, *do not travel*. To do so would lead to trouble.

FIVE TRAVEL REQUIREMENTS

1. Know where you are and where you are going. If you don't know . . . stay put.
2. Have some method of finding your direction—for example, a compass. If you don't have an accurate means of doing this . . . stay put.
3. Know your physical capabilities. If in doubt . . . stay put.
4. Consider your clothing. Do you have the correct clothing for the conditions you may encounter? Do you have proper footwear for the terrain you'll be covering? Unless you are outfitted properly . . . stay put.
5. Your water, food, fuel, shelter and methods of signalling must be considered in relation to the type of country that you are in, as well as the weather. If it looks like you are walking into a more difficult situation . . . stay put.

Always conserve your energy. Think about your predicament, plan carefully and set realistic goals to improve upon your situation.

TRAVEL TIPS

Once you have met the five travel requirements and are convinced that a move will improve your situation, you will have the confidence to relax and plan your journey. Wilderness travel is relatively easy if you observe the following points.

- **Choose a direction that you think will improve your situation.** Try to get to high ground to pick a landmark. (You can climb a tree, but test each branch carefully so that you don't have an accident.) Use your compass and, if you have them, binoculars to assist you in choosing your direction.
- **Game trails may provide a path through bush country.** The main game trails follow ridges and river flats and are connected by a network of smaller trails. The danger in following these trails is that you may encounter animals—see chapter 13 on bears. Also, unless you keep a careful check on direction, you may wander off your heading.
- **Streams may be followed to rivers or lakes where you may find habitation.** Generally, it is better to follow the drainage pattern than to cross it. The winding nature of rivers usually means travelling about four times farther to get from A to B than if you were travelling along ridges. Unless the waterways in the area are well known to you, building a raft is not recommended.
- **Ridges offer drier, more insect-free travel than bottom land.** There will usually be less underbrush, and as a result it will be easier to see and be seen.
- **River crossings should be attempted only when absolutely necessary.** As a rule of thumb, fast-moving water deeper than knee height calls for extreme caution. If you cannot remember crossing it before and can find another route, avoid the crossing.
- **If you must cross a moving body of water, it is best to do so in the morning,** when the stream flow is usually lower as a

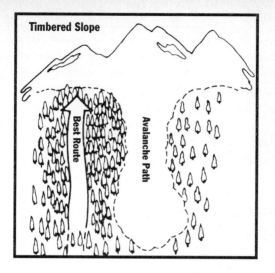

result of night cooling. Remove all your clothing, bundle it up and try to keep it dry. Take off your socks, but wear your boots to protect your feet and to give secure footing. If forced to swim in a fast-flowing river, start upstream from your proposed landing place and let the current drift you down. When crossing a fast, shallow stream, use a pole to help maintain your footing by placing the butt-end down on the upstream side.

- **Decide whether to cross or to go around a lake.** If you decide to cross, use a raft or flotation gear to assist you. Swimming cold waters can be risky. Play it safe.
- **Deadfall and swamps should be avoided.** Deadfall can be dangerous because of the ever-present danger of slipping and causing injury. Walking through swamps will steadily sap your strength and you may get wet feet; go around them.
- **Mountains have their own particular problems.** Watch for overhead threats, shale slides, broken ground due to wildlife burrows and lava beds that are sharp and dangerous. When a

group is crossing unstable surfaces, it is advisable to rope the party together and send one person at a time across the area. The rest of the group acts as an anchor against a possible slide. In early spring, cross mountain streams in early morning to avoid the greatest volume of water, which occurs when the sun melts the snow. In summer the snow line may be high above the stream, but it can still significantly affect the water volume. When crossing snow slopes in summer, it is less dangerous to cross early in the morning when they have a hard crust.

WINTER TRAVEL

Game trails, especially if heavily used, will save walking through deep snow, but you must avoid being led off the direction of your planned route. Streams and rivers, the highways of the Canadian north, will provide your best route. There are, however, dangers in winter river travel that must be avoided. For example, in certain areas of a river, weak ice will be found.

TIPS FOR TRAVELLING ON ICE

1. **Stay away from rocks and other protrusions,** since ice formation in these localities will have been retarded by eddies.
2. **Walk on the inside of curves,** since on the outside of a curve the river current has an eroding effect on the underside of the ice surface.
3. **At the junction of two rivers,** head to the bank or walk on the opposite side of the join because the currents from both rivers hold up the formation of the ice through turbulence.
4. **Stay on clear ice when possible,** since a deep layer of snow will insulate and retard freezing, and erosion by the river may leave only a snow bridge.
5. **Carry a pole for testing ice.** It should be light enough to be carried comfortably but heavy enough to support your

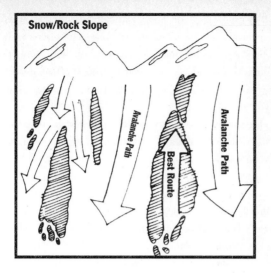

weight. Test the ice by tapping it. You want to hear a solid sound, which indicates a safe surface to walk on. A "hollow drum" sound indicates that the ice is probably too thin to support you, and a crackly sound signifies thin ice on top of thicker ice.

6. **When crossing ice in a group, spread out and go in single file.** This formation distributes the weight over a greater surface, lessening chances of a breakthrough and increasing chances of assisting anyone who does break through. The leader should test the ice by tapping it.

7. **Be prepared to get rid of your pack if you should fall through the ice.** Have the hip belt of your pack unbuckled when you cross ice so that if you fall through, you can slip your pack off.

8. **Before beginning any trip on ice, be certain that a good waterproof, fire-starting kit is immediately available.** Carry one in a closed pocket as well as in your pack.

9. **If you fall through the ice, don't panic.** Roll over on your back as soon as you are in the water and work your way to the edge of the solid ice. Put your elbows up on the ice behind you and carefully edge the rest of your body onto the solid ice. Keep crawling backwards until you are certain that you are on safe ice.

10. **Once you are out of the water, your first act is to head for the nearest snowbank and roll in it.** Light, powdery snow is an excellent blotter and will soak up most of the excess water. The snow that adheres to your clothing will provide an insulating effect while you or your companion builds a fire. If you are alone, move quickly and build a fire before you become too numb to move your fingers and before your clothes freeze solid.

    Be aware that once you have a beaten trail across ice on a lake, it does not assure you of a safe crossing in the future. The fact that you have compacted the snow reduces some of its insulating qualities. As long as the weather remains cold, the frost penetrating through the packed snow of your trail could cancel out the effects of any erosion of the under surface of the ice by a warm current. When the temperature rises and there is no longer frost, however, the current causes gradual erosion. Where the ice on a lake is covered by a few metres of snow that prevent the frost from penetrating to the ice, a good deal of caution should be exercised. Check several routes to make sure that you are choosing the safest one.

11. **River ice can be even more treacherous,** since the current eroding the under surface of the ice is much stronger and a greater volume of warm water is brought in contact with the ice. Take extra caution on snow-covered river ice. Glare ice will generally offer a safe crossing. To lessen the danger, wear snowshoes or skis, which give better weight distribution than wearing only boots. Be ready to quickly kick them off should you break through the ice.

12. **You may encounter overflow under the snow.** Wet feet freeze rapidly.
13. **When travelling on snow, water or ice, wear sunglasses to protect your eyes from the reflected glare.** If you don't have sunglasses, make a pair by cutting small eye-slits into a piece of wood and securing it to your head (see chapter 3).

TIPS FOR TRAVELLING IN THE MOUNTAINS

1. **Ridges present easier walking conditions,** since they usually have less snow than valleys.
2. **Mountain areas,** particularly in winter, can be treacherous, since there is the possibility of snow slides, uncertain footing and sudden storms. Snow slides will occur from natural causes, but care should be taken to avoid causing them through carelessness. Whenever snowfall is heavy, suspect avalanche conditions. Factors that contribute to possible avalanches are a slope of 20 to 50 degrees with a heavy snowfall on it; rain or rising temperature can increase the risk in these areas, as does the heat of the sun. Caution is advised. Avoid crossing avalanche chutes. If possible, avoid travelling the day after a heavy snowfall.
3. **When walking in heavy snow on a sloped area,** if you find your footprints are leaving larger than normal depressions—perhaps twice as large as your footprint—you are in a potentially dangerous region.
4. **Before attempting a winter trip,** inquire about snow conditions from those who know the area well. Snow depth, snow consistency, air temperature and snow consolidation offer valuable information about avalanche dangers.
5. **Deadfall is even more dangerous in winter than in summer,** since a lot of it will be covered by snow, making walking conditions treacherous. The accompanying sketches will help you choose the best route to travel while in snowy, mountainous regions.

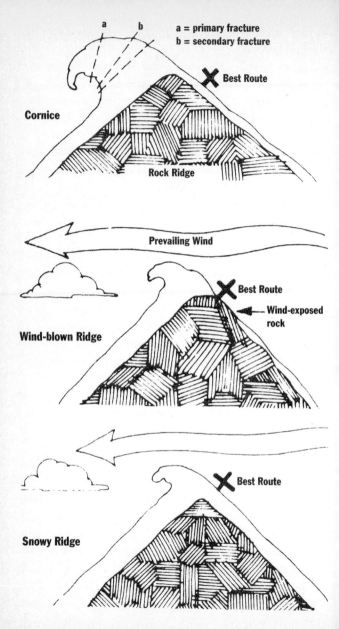

a = primary fracture
b = secondary fracture

X Best Route

Cornice

Rock Ridge

Prevailing Wind

X Best Route

Wind-exposed rock

Wind-blown Ridge

X Best Route

Snowy Ridge

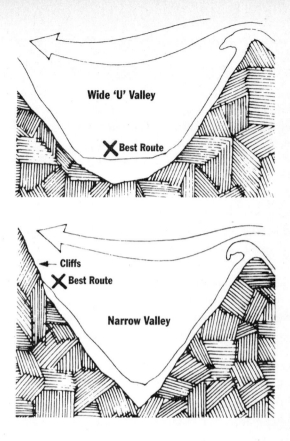

KEEPING WARM

One of the most important things to learn about living outside during winter is how to keep warm. The principles of keeping warm can be remembered by the catch word COLD.

C — Keep your clothing **Clean**.
O — Avoid **Overheating**.
L — Wear your clothing **Loose** and in **Layers**.
D — Keep your clothing **Dry**.

It is important to keep your clothing clean, since dirt blocks air spaces. In addition, if you get a cut, you want things to be clean.

To stay warm, avoid overheating your body, which causes perspiration and eventually leads to heat loss (see chapter 3). Overheating is best controlled by slowing down, by providing ventilation and by removing layers. You can remove your mitts, push back your hood, open your jacket partially and loosen it at the waist. In addition, open your pants at the cuffs and at the waist and open the sleeves of your jacket at the wrists. You can also remove one layer—for example, a shirt or fleece vest—to avoid overheating. Pump air through your clothing by opening your jacket or shirt and fanning yourself with the garment.

Moisture can soak into your clothes from two sources—from melting snow and frost that has collected on the outside of your clothing and from your own perspiration on the inside. When entering any heated shelter or vehicle, remember to brush or shake all snow and frost from your clothes. Take advantage of every available opportunity to dry out your clothes. Here are some suggestions:

1. **Drying footwear.** Careful boot drying is important. Prop your boots up facing the fire but not too close; check them often to make sure that they aren't cracking or shrinking. Wet boots are better than boots deformed from improper drying. Don't warm your feet in front of the fire while wearing footwear. Your footwear will burn long before your feet become warm.
2. **Drying wet clothing.** Hang each item separately. Don't hang things directly over the fire; they may fall down. Don't place anything too close to the fire. Nylon melts easily and wool quickly becomes scorched; scorched clothing has no heat retention. Don't hang clothes over steaming pots.

   When it is not possible to dry clothing indoors in subfreezing temperatures, hanging it outdoors in the cold helps. When it has frozen, beat out the frost and ice. Although this technique will not give you a completely dry garment, it will get rid of much of the moisture and make it possible to quickly dry out what remains.

3. **Drying damp clothing.** As you walk, damp clothing can be draped over your backpack to dry. It can also be placed under your pack close to your body. Don't place damp clothing in your sleeping bag to dry. This only transfers moisture from your damp clothing into the inside of your sleeping bag. If something is almost dry, however, you can put it in the sleeping bag with you at night and it will finish drying. Take every opportunity to dry your clothes. Your comfort and possibly your life will depend on having dry clothes. To keep warm, remember the code word COLD.

IMPROVISED SNOWSHOES

It is much easier to walk on top of snow rather than through it. Snowshoes work well. If you don't have a pair, improvise. A simple

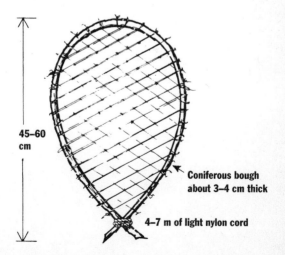

45–60 cm

Coniferous bough about 3–4 cm thick

4–7 m of light nylon cord

bear-paw snowshoe can be made by bending any long green sapling bough into a snowshoe shape. Use small sticks and twine to make the centre of the shoe and fasten it with rope, string, wire or perhaps even a root. Use your ingenuity . . . it can mean survival.

MEASURING DISTANCE

A simple means of determining distance is an asset when trying to orient yourself on a map or when surveying your survival site and exploring its full potential.

One method of estimating distance is the tally-and-pace system. It is based on the 75-cm pace. This is neither a long nor a short pace for most people; it is more like an everyday stride. Remember, when you walk uphill, you tend to take a longer pace; walking downhill, you take a shorter pace. You will need to allow for this difference.

- 1 pace = 75 cm
- 1 double pace (each time the same foot touches the ground) = 150 cm = 1.5 m
- 66 double paces = 99 m = 1 tally (tie a knot in a string for each tally)
- 10 tallies = approximately 1000 m or 1 km

13 <u>BEARS</u>

British Columbia is bear country. Approximately half of the population of grizzly bears and a quarter of the total of black bears in Canada live in this province. In the wilderness you are in their territory—respect them and be aware of their behavioral patterns. Bears, like people, are all different, and every bear encounter is unique. This chapter presents guidelines only; your common sense and judgement will play an important role in determining what you should do if you meet a bear.

It is *always* best to avoid a bear, and even if you see one from a distance, be cautious. Sometimes a bear encounter is unavoidable, and since the species vary in behaviour, it is best to identify which species you are dealing with. A grizzly may be black, brown, blond or silver tipped; it has an upturned muzzle, a concave face and a hump on its shoulders. A black bear may be varying shades from black to blond, has a straighter face and is generally smaller.

BEAR SIGNS
Telltale signs that you are in bear country are tracks, scat, rotten wood that has been torn apart, earth that has been dug up, bits of hair on trees, carcasses of other animals (which may be partially buried under dirt or leaves) and an area with lots of ripe berries. Bears tend to stay near their food supply, so if it looks as if one has been feeding, it is probably still around. Leave the area and don't camp anywhere nearby.

TO AVOID BEARS
Bears have an acute sense of smell and hearing. When in the wilderness:

1. Make noise, such as talking loudly or clapping, so that they are aware of your presence. You don't want to startle a bear.

2. Don't camp on or near game trails or close to streams.

3. At your camp, pitch tents in a semicircle or a line so that if a bear arrives, it can easily leave; suspend food from trees at least 4 m above the ground and about 100 m downwind from your tents; keep all food and garbage away from sleeping areas; put all food and any fragrant items, such as soap, in the tree stash. Keep your camp clean. If possible, pack your garbage out. If you must burn refuse with a food odour, do so in a *hot* campfire (heat reduces the burning-garbage smell).

SHOULD YOU ENCOUNTER A BEAR

Most bear attacks occur because the bear is surprised—it may be protecting its cubs or perhaps has been interrupted while feeding. You have no chance of outrunning a bear, since it travels at about 14 m per second. Also, it is a myth that bears cannot run downhill; they can run down steep slopes with agility. If you encounter a bear, take the following steps:

1. Try to remain calm and move quietly away, walking cautiously backwards.

2. If you feel that the bear has not detected you but is moving towards you, get out of its path.

3. If the bear has noticed you, make noise but don't shout; move slowly away.

4. Should the bear follow, set something down on the trail to distract it, but don't leave food.

On occasion, black bears have stalked people. (If the bear has come to associate people with food, this is a dangerous situation.) If leaving the scene has not worked and the bear is acting aggressively, you might try these tactics:

1. Wave your arms, jump up and down, make noise and appear aggressive.

2. Move upwind to give the bear your scent. Once the bear has identified what you are, it is usually not interested in you.

3. If the bear stands on hind legs and moves its head back and forth, it is trying to get your scent to identify you. It does not attack on its hind legs.

4. A bear charges on all fours. Often it will bluff an attack and stop 2 to 3 m in front of you.

5. If a grizzly attacks you, play dead by lying on your side in the fetal position, head between your knees, arms over your head with fingers tightly laced; remain in a tight ball.

6. If there is time during a grizzly attack, you can climb a tree. You must get at least 4 m high.

7. If a black bear attacks you, fight it with anything you can—for example, a hiking stick, a shovel, heavy branches or stones.

8. Bear spray or pepper spray may be used during a bear attack, but keep the following in mind:

    (a) you must be within 3 m of the bear;

    (b) do not use it against the wind. You must get in a position to spray the bear with the wind at your back; if you are spraying against the wind, it may temporarily incapacitate you. You must also make sure that you have a reliable product and know how to use it.

14 SIGNALLING

In order to be rescued, you must make sure that rescuers can see you. Signalling your position and, in some situations, what you require, is imperative to assist with your rescue.

FIRE

The age-old signals are smoke during the day and fire by night. And these tried-and-true methods can still be used. Lay three signal fires about 30 m apart and have them ready to ignite as soon as you see or hear an aircraft. (Three of anything—for example, three whistle blows or three gunshots—is an internationally recognized distress signal.)

In a heavily wooded region, look for a clearing to set the fires (see chapter 6). Smoke will not be easily noticed in wind, rain or snow. On a clear day, however, it may be spotted from a fire lookout or spotter plane. Add oil-soaked rags, plastic or rubber to a fire to create dark smoke (best on overcast days) and use moss, ferns and green leaves for a light smoke, which is distinguishable against blue skies. Always use extreme care with fire.

FLARES

If emergency flares are part of your survival kit, make sure that you know how to use them. Follow instructions carefully. In a forested area, red flares will be easily spotted; over snow either red or green will be seen. Flares can be seen for kilometres, but always have backup signals ready after setting a flare off. Also, flares have a shelf life, so check the expiry date before taking them on a trip.

MORSE CODE

The International Morse Code emergency distress signal of sos (Save Our Souls) is signalled by using dots and dashes:

. . . – – – . . . The dashes are twice as long as the dots, so the code is three short, three long and three more short. The code can be signalled using a flashlight at night when you have some hope that it will be seen. Don't waste the batteries unless you hear an aircraft. sos can also be signalled with a whistle or by radio.

GROUND SIGNALS

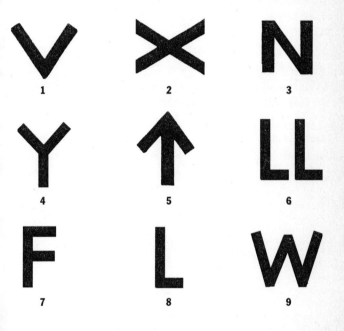

Key

1. Require assistance.
2. Require medical assistance.
3. No or negative.
4. Yes or affirmative.
5. Proceeding in this direction.
6. All is well.
7. Require food and water.
8. Require fuel and oil.
9. Need repairs.

Easy-to-construct ground signals can be seen well from the air during daylight, and they work for you unattended. Lay them on open, even ground if possible. If you have marker panels in your survival kit, use them. If not, parachute cloth, branches or piles of rocks will work. Try to provide good colour contrast between the symbols and the background. In snow, tramp out trenches to form signal letters. Outline them with pieces of bark or fir branches placed on top of the snow near the edge of the trench. These give excellent shadow effects and colour contrast. The recommended size of each signal is about 10 m long and 3 m wide with about 3 m between symbols.

SIGNAL MIRROR

This is an effective method of signalling for rescue. During hours of sunlight, flash the double-sided mirror (or reflective object) along the horizon, even though you may not have any indication that a plane is in the area. Search craft have turned towards a mirror flash even though survivors have not heard or seen them.

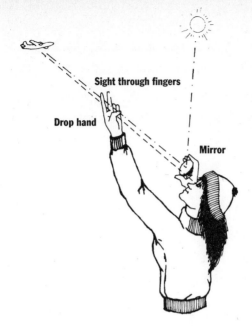

Sight through fingers

Drop hand

Mirror

After your signal has been acknowledged, do not continue to flash the mirror, because it may be blinding to the pilot. Flash it only occasionally to assist in keeping the search plane on course.

If you don't have a signal mirror (some Silva compasses have mirrors with them), you can make one from any shiny material—for example, a piece of aluminum foil, a tin can or part of an aircraft. The mirror must have a hole in the middle. If you are using a mirror, attempt to scratch a spot through from the back. When using foil, you can simply poke a hole through.

To send signals: Hold the mirror a few centimetres from your face and take a sight at an airplane through the hole and in the direction of the sun. (If you have not spotted an aircraft, sweep the horizon slowly in the hope that someone will pick up your signal.) The sun should shine through the hole, and you will see a spot of light on your face. To ensure that you have the mirror in the correct position, adjust the angle so that this spot of light disappears back through the hole in the mirror.

If you have difficulty adjusting the mirror's position, move the mirror close to your eyes and line your hand up between you and the aircraft. Adjust the angle of the mirror to flash on your hand and then move your hand away. This method, shown in the second diagram, is the best one if you don't have a mirror with a hole in it.

15 <u>HYPOTHERMIA</u>

Clinically defined as a "significant decrease in body temperature," hypothermia is the enemy of outdoorspeople. When your body becomes chilled to the degree that heat loss exceeds heat production, symptoms of hypothermia begin to appear. The probability of hypothermia increases as the temperature decreases, and the severity of it depends on the degree of coldness and length of exposure time.

Many people think of hypothermia as happening after a fall into cold water, but it can also occur when you are improperly dressed and get caught in cold, wet, windy conditions. Hypothermia often occurs in temperatures between 5° and 10° C. This chapter deals with hypothermia caused by exposure to cold, wet, windy weather and hypothermia due to immersion in cold water. It incorporates information from the latest research done at the University of Victoria.

HYPOTHERMIA DUE TO EXPOSURE
TO COLD, WET, WINDY CONDITIONS

Hypothermia can occur in any season, climate and location. Consider this scenario. You and a companion hike through a sunny valley to arrive at a mountain ridge, where you encounter rain and wind. The end of the trail is 5 km away, and your lightweight jacket and pants become wet. Your hands and feet become cold, and you begin to shiver. Just before arriving at your destination, your movements become sluggish and your thinking unclear. At the hike's conclusion, your companion assists you into the vehicle and wraps you in a blanket, and gradually your body warms. You are one of the lucky ones. Although you were suffering the first symptoms of hypothermia, good luck may have saved your life.

Be prepared

With the exception of cases involving injuries, hypothermia can usually be avoided by taking the following steps:

1. Check the weather. If conditions are severe, cancel the outing. Never head into bad weather.
2. Take appropriate clothing. Waterproof and windproof gear as well as something warm is a good idea on any hike. What you take obviously depends on the length of the trip and the time of year—use your common sense.
3. Take a simple emergency shelter—for example, a plastic sheet and string.
4. Take equipment such as waterproof matches, a knife and a flashlight; these items can mean the difference between survival and disaster. You also need to know how to use your equipment—it's no use having matches if you don't know how to build a fire.
5. Take emergency food and water.
6. Group leaders must make decisions and take charge. This means ensuring that everyone has appropriate clothing and that you have some form of shelter, a means of making hot drinks, a first-aid kit and water. Group leaders must make sure that everyone stays together and stops for energy-efficient snacks. Leaders should also be aware of signs of fatigue and discomfort among group members; people will often deny that they are in trouble.

Although there are symptoms that are specific to hypothermia, everyone reacts to cold stress differently. It is important to react to the early signs of hypothermia, but since you don't have a thermometer to check a person's body temperature, it is often difficult to read the symptoms. Keep alert; if warning signs are spotted and measures taken, tragedy can be avoided.

Symptoms and treatment of exposure

1. Hands and feet become cold and then the rest of your body becomes chilled. To warm hands and feet, move your arms and legs. Keeping the big muscles moving creates heat. Be cautious; when your body cools, you lose some dexterity. Also, people tend to be distracted by cold and may wander off course. Note: Experts advise that this stage may or may not actually be hypothermia, but it is worth taking precautions and monitoring carefully. Symptoms of **mild hypothermia** are complaining of cold, shivering, slurring your words and showing no interest in the situation. To treat mild hypothermia:

   - Stop travelling. Research shows that people who take shelter before becoming exhausted are more likely to survive than those who walk until they are exhausted. If the weather is bad, get out of the wind and rain and assume a HELP position. This Heat Escape Lessening Posture is a sitting, fetal position with your arms wrapped tightly around your bent legs. Huddle together if you're in a group.
   - If you can, remove wet clothing and replace it with dry clothing. Make sure the person is wearing hat and mitts and that his or her jacket is properly closed.
   - Supply high-energy food and a sweet, warm, noncaffeine beverage.
   - Allow shivering to continue, since it is the best way to restore the body's temperature.
   - Wrap the person in an extra blanket or a space blanket, or if nothing else is available, wrap tarp or plastic bags around the person to help retain body heat. Make sure the person is not sitting on the cold ground.

   All of the above are steps in **passive rewarming**, which means preventing further heat loss and allowing the casualty's body to rewarm itself.

2. Signs of **moderate hypothermia** are violent shivering or cessation of shivering, confusion, clumsiness, sleepiness, muscle stiffness, and perhaps a slow breath and pulse rate. There may also be dilated pupils. Note: Cessation of shivering indicates a serious problem. Treatment of moderate hypothermia is the same as for mild hypothermia. In addition:

- Avoid rough handling and do not let the person walk.
- Do not give anything to drink, since the casualty's muscles for swallowing may not be working and he or she could choke.

Active rewarming means adding heat to a person's body. It can cause complications, however, and, ideally, should be done in a hospital. The effectiveness of methods that have been used in the past—for example, skin-to-skin contact and warming a person's body using hot water bottles—has not been proved, and such methods can lead to complications. When in doubt *act conservatively*.

Although it has not been proven that skin-to-skin contact will rewarm a casualty, it is a method that is still tried. Two people strip to underclothes and huddle in a sleeping bag until the casualty begins to warm. Take care that the rescuer does not become overly cold; exchange positions with another person who is not suffering from hypothermia. You would change with another person before becoming chilled.

3. **Severe hypothermia** can quickly follow moderate hypothermia. If the person is barely conscious or unconscious and has slow, shallow breathing and a weak, slow pulse as well as pale, very cold, perhaps bluish skin, he or she is in the last stages of hypothermia. Note: Some casualties may appear to be dead, but there may be a faint, slow heartbeat. Continue to treat. To treat severe hypothermia:

- Handle the victim gently.
- Prevent further heat loss.
- Move the casualty with great care to gain medical assistance if it can be obtained within a few hours.
- Call for emergency aid.
- Keep the person warm and let him or her recover slowly.
- Never rub or warm hands, feet, arms or legs, since moving these limbs needlessly may cause cold blood to be circulated back to the heart. Note: Once a person begins to warm, he or she may ask to have limbs warmed—*don't do this*. Allow them to warm gradually. Also, as the person recovers, do not give anything by mouth until you are sure the person is fully coherent. Keep the person resting.

4. If the person is unconscious, attempt to find a pulse at the neck (carotid) for at least 1 or 2 minutes. Feel and listen for breathing—watch for chest movement and put your ear next to the person's nose and mouth. To treat an unconscious person:

- Start rescue breathing (see chapter 16).
- Prevent further heat loss.
- Handle the person gently.
- Get medical care.

HYPOTHERMIA DUE TO
IMMERSION IN COLD WATER

Immersion in cold water puts you in danger of hypothermia, and British Columbia has a lot of cold water. A plunge into "cold" water (usually defined as colder than 25° C) cools the skin and peripheral tissues within a few minutes, but it takes 10 to 15 minutes before the temperature of the heart, brain and internal organs begins to drop. Note: Isolated cases of sudden death have been reported from falls into cold water. The causes are unclear but may have been from a heart attack due to a change in blood pressure accompanied by immersion in cold water. In addition, hyperventilation (overbreathing), when prolonged, can lead to unconsciousness and drowning.

It is important that boaters and others at risk of accidental immersion in cold water be aware of the factors that determine the rate of body cooling. Such knowledge helps prevent accidents and improves chances of survival if a mishap does occur. The variables that affect survival in cold water are water temperature, the survivor's physique, the type of protective clothing worn, the state of the water (rough or calm), the survivor's behaviour in water and the amount of the survivor's body that is immersed in water.

The accompanying graph shows the average predicted survival times of average-size adults in water of different low temperatures. These figures are based on experimental cooling of men and women who were holding still in ocean water and wearing a standard life-jacket and light clothing. As indicated, the predicted survival time is 2½ to 3 hours in water of 10° C. Survival time is increased by extra body fat and decreased by small body size.

Although women usually have slightly more body fat, they cool faster because of their usually smaller body size. Children cool much faster than adults (see number 6 under "Survival Strategies" below).

Preparation
Again, the right equipment and knowledge can help you survive if you are immersed in cold water.

1. **Protective clothing.** If you are in a sinking boat and have time, put on several woollen sweaters and extra pants to increase your insulation. Cover these layers with a winter jacket tied between the legs to keep it from floating up and then put on a Personal Flotation Device. Tuck pants into sock tops. Wear a

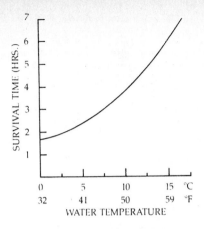

hat. The areas of the body that have high rates of heat loss are the head, neck, sides of the chest and groin region.

2. **Personal Flotation Device.** PFDs allow you to keep afloat. There is a variety of styles of vest-type, foam-filled PFDs. Choose one that is Canadian Coast Guard Approved, can be adjusted to fit properly and has insulative, closed-cell foam between the inner and outer layers of fabric.

There are also floater jackets and full-body survival suits

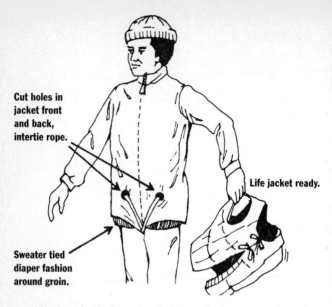

Cut holes in jacket front and back, intertie rope.

Life jacket ready.

Sweater tied diaper fashion around groin.

with closed-cell foam insulation and closures at the wrists, thighs and ankles. Some have extras such as an inflatable head support pillow that give additional buoyancy.

Survival strategies

Use the following techniques to maximize your chances of surviving a cold-water spill.

1. **Do not panic.** It is important to remain calm in a cold-water emergency. If possible, enter the water gradually and try to control your breathing. The more clothing and insulation your body has, the less will be the initial shock on entry. Thrashing about and hyperventilating enhance cooling and increase the probability that you will inhale water (drown).

2. **Use HELP and huddle.** The two techniques that reduce heat loss and add to survival time when you are wearing a PFD are HELP and huddle.

(a) **HELP (Heat Escape Lessening Postures).** Hold the inner sides of the arms tightly against the sides of the chest; this position secures the PFD tightly against your body. Press thighs together and raise legs to close off the groin region. Try to stay in this fetal position and minimize movement. Note: If your PFD prevents a tight fetal position, keep your thighs and lower legs together as much as possible. Be careful not to tip the back of your head into the water, since this position adds to the cooling of the brain. The HELP body position can result in a one-third increase in potential survival time.

HELP

(b) **Huddle.** Two or more people in cold water should wrap their arms around each other's shoulders and maximize body contact by pulling their chests and bodies close together. This huddle position increases potential survival time by one-third.

3. **If you have no flotation device,** there are two anti-drowning techniques to adopt.

   (a) **Treading water.** Continuously moving your arms and legs in various patterns to keep your head out of the water. Research shows that subjects treading water had an

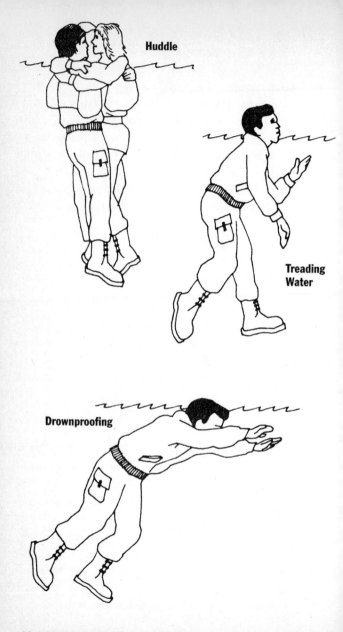

Huddle

Treading Water

Drownproofing

average cooling rate that was 33 per cent faster than those holding still wearing a PFD.

(b) **Drownproofing.** Fill your lungs with air, adopt a restful floating position with arms forward and every 10 to 15 seconds raise your head for air. In warm water (the average summer temperature in some lakes is 17° to 20°C), even nonswimmers can avoid drowning for several hours using this method. Unfortunately, it does not work well in cold water. In experiments in ocean water with a temperature of 10°C, subjects had a body cooling rate that was 82 per cent faster than that of a person holding still and wearing a PFD.

4. **Get out of the water.** In almost all weather, out of the water is better than in. If it is possible to climb on top of an overturned boat, do so. If immersion is unavoidable, the less of your body that is exposed to the water, the better.

5. **Do not swim.** In cold water, more heat is lost from swimming as a result of increased blood circulation to the arms, legs and skin than from holding still. Research shows that the average person swimming in a PFD cools 33 per cent faster than when holding still. It is only considered safe to swim if the shore is within an estimated .75 km and there are no large waves or strong current. This is a difficult decision under emergency conditions.

6. **Give special protection** to children. In addition to being smaller, children generally have less fat than adults. These two factors make them particularly vulnerable to cold water. If a family is immersed, it is important for the parents to either get the children partially or completely out of the water or get them onto some form of flotation—for example, an overturned boat. If no flotation is available, the adults should get in a huddle position with the children between them. This position will minimize heat loss and maximize insulation.

Hypothermia first aid for immersion in cold water

Get the person out of the water and replace wet clothing. The method of treatment depends on the degree of hypothermia evident. If the victim is conscious, talking clearly and sensibly, and shivering vigorously, then provide a dry environment (put the person in a sleeping bag or cover with a blanket) and a warm drink. (Do not give alcohol, since it accelerates heat loss from the body.) Treat hypothermia symptoms as outlined in "Symptoms and Survival Strategies" earlier in this chapter.

In conclusion, it should be noted that because of variations in water conditions, weather conditions and people's body builds, swimming ability and clothing, survival time of individuals varies. The information in this chapter should therefore be considered a guideline only.

16 <u>HEALTH AND FIRST AID</u>

The instructions and treatments given in this chapter are focussed on aid that should be given in the absence of medical help. The information in this chapter does not replace a doctor's care, but it does cover the most common emergency health situations that you may encounter in the backcountry. If you plan to go into the wilderness, it is essential that you complete a first-aid course and that you keep your training current. Always take a first-aid kit and book with you on a trip.

PREVENTION

Avoiding sickness and injury in the wilderness begins at home. You should be in good health and physical condition before a trip. Make sure that you are prepared for any emergency. For example, poor footwear can result in a bad sprain; using a shampoo with a fragrance can attract stinging insects. Consider every detail.

Once in the backcountry, try to maintain a balanced diet. Several small meals are more energy-efficient than a few large ones. Vitamins A, C and D are essential. Vitamin A can be ingested by eating fish, vegetables and dairy products. Vitamin C strengthens your resistance. In the wilderness it can be found in Oregon grape and mountain sorrel, among other plants. Vitamin D helps fight infection and promotes healing. It is found in fish liver oil and some raw greens (see chapter 9).

Even when it is difficult, keep yourself clean. (Soap can be made by boiling the inner bark of a pine tree.) Washing before preparing food can mean avoiding diarrhea.

TAKING CHARGE

Wilderness first aid presents many challenges and it often calls for difficult decision making that may mean the difference between life and death. If someone suffers from a stomach ache, the group leader must decide whether the situation is serious enough to return to civilization or if it is a case of traveller's stomach that will soon pass. The group leader should be familiar with first-aid practices and be able to make this decision.

Make sure that you understand the instructions on all medication that you are carrying. Be aware of common symptoms and injuries that may be incurred in the wilderness and watch for them in yourself and in others. Take the time to be certain of what you are treating. Whenever possible, obtain medical advice by radio before giving medicine and check with the patient regarding allergies to medication. Keep careful records of when medication is administered.

BASIC FIRST AID

Regardless of the injury, there are certain basics that apply when treating people, including those in the wilderness. The priority list is:

1. Check breathing problems and clear airway.
2. Stop any bleeding.
3. Protect the person from the cold.
4. Check for dehydration.
5. Treat for shock.

BREATHING PROBLEMS

If you cannot detect breathing when you put your ear to the injured person's face, check for airway blockage. If you don't see a blockage, try to open the airway by doing the following:

1. **If you do not suspect head and neck injury,** place a hand on the casualty's forehead and, with your fingers under the chin bone, gently tip the head back. This head tilt–chin lift draws

the tongue up and out of the airway; this blockage may be the only problem.

2. **If you suspect head and neck injury,** protect the neck. Lift the jaw forward and upward by placing your fingers behind the angle of the jaw and your thumbs on the casualty's cheek-bones. Thrust the jaw forward and upward. Steady the head with your palms and wrists. The jaw thrust lifts the tongue from the airway. Note: Many injured people have died because they have been left lying on their backs. When the injured person becomes unconscious, the tongue relaxes and blocks the air passage. The recovery or drainage position allows fluids to drain from the body and is one of the most important and basic parts of first aid. To place a person in the recovery position you must

1. cross the casualty's legs at the ankles, far side on top;
2. place the near arm along the casualty's side, the far arm across the chest;
3. support the head with one hand and grip the clothing at the waist on the far side with your other hand;
4. roll the person gently towards you, protecting head and neck, and rest the casualty against your knees;
5. bend the person's upper knee towards you to form a support;
6. position the head with chin slightly extended to keep airway open;
7. place the casualty's upper arm out from the body and bent for support to keep the person from rolling onto his or her face;
8. place the lower arm along the person's back to prevent the person from rolling onto his or her back.

If the casualty is on snow, place him or her on a bedroll, or some other item, to give protection from the snow. Note: Do not put a casualty that you suspect of having a spinal injury in this position.

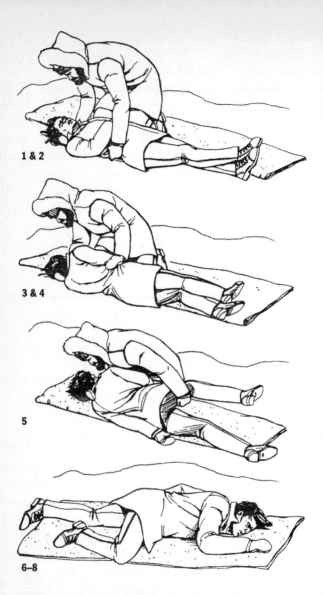

1 & 2

3 & 4

5

6–8

Recovery or Drainage Position

If the person is having a breathing problem, a sitting-up or semi-sitting-up position is best as long as there is no head, neck or spinal injury. Using blankets and a sleep roll as padding, lean the person against a rock or hillside. This position opens up the airway and makes breathing easier.

If breathing has stopped
When someone stops breathing, you must give mouth-to-mouth ventilation. Follow these steps:

1. Use one hand to maintain the chin lift and the other to pinch the casualty's nose shut.

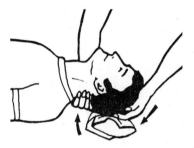

2. Cover the person's mouth with your own, making a tight seal.
3. Breathe air slowly into the casualty's lungs, taking 1½ to 2 seconds to ventilate.

4. Move your mouth away to let the air rush out. To be sure that the air is exchanged, listen, feel and watch carefully.

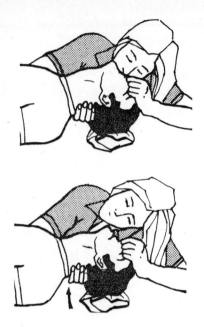

5. Repeat the cycle every 5 seconds for an adult casualty.
6. Check for pulse—there is an artery on either side of the neck. Do not compress both sides at the same time.

HOW TO STOP BLEEDING

After establishing that the casualty is breathing, you must stop any bleeding. Blood loss leads to shock and infection. The following steps will control all but the most severe cases of bleeding; all can be performed at the same time.

1. **Direct pressure.** If a thick cloth is available, press directly on the wound. (Make sure that nothing is embedded in the wound.) If possible, this cloth should be a sterile bandage. In

the case of severe bleeding, it may be necessary to use whatever you have. Do not keep checking to see if bleeding has stopped. Eventually the blood flow will stop and clots will form. (If the cloth becomes soaked through, don't remove; add another layer and continue pressing.)

2. **Elevation.** While keeping pressure on the wound, elevate the injured part, if no fractures are present. If possible, elevate above the level of the heart, thus slowing the blood flow to the injury.

3. **Rest.** Place the person at rest so that the pulse will slow and less blood will be pumped. Once the bleeding is stopped, bandage the wound. Make frequent checks for circulation. If toes or fingers appear blue or numb, loosen dressing.

If this method does not stop the bleeding and *the situation is life-threatening*, use a tourniquet. This is a band applied around the injured limb so tightly that all blood flow beyond is cut off. The tourniquet should be wide and flat (a soft strap or piece of rolled-up garbage bag will work) and should be placed above the wound as close to it as possible. Wrap the tourniquet around twice, tie a half-knot, place a small stick over the half-knot and tie a full knot. Twist to tighten until bleeding stops and then tie the stick in place. Note the time the tourniquet was applied. Leave it in place if medical assistance is less than one hour away. If more than an hour is anticipated, loosen the tourniquet briefly at the end of each 45 minutes and apply direct pressure to the wound. (You need to let some blood go to the injured limb. This step does not apply if the casualty has lost a limb.) Note: A tourniquet is a last resort. Any casualty treated with a tourniquet must be taken for medical treatment as soon as possible.

To treat a minor wound, clean carefully and apply a sterile dressing. Do not touch the wound. Keep the dressing clean. Note: Because of the danger of HIV, hepatitis and other bacterial infections, always wear gloves when treating an injury.

Protect from the cold. A sick or injured person is more vulnerable to cold than a healthy person. Cover the casualty with a sleeping bag and remember to put something *underneath* the person's body as well (see chapter 15).

DEHYDRATION

Dehydration occurs when the body loses more water than it takes in. When you are in the wilderness and exerting yourself, it is important to drink a lot of liquids. Do not drink alcohol or beverages containing caffeine, since they increase dehydration. Symptoms are dry tongue, thirst, tiredness, nausea and sleepiness. Dehydration can eventually lead to shock. To treat:

1. Give water, salt and water (about 5 ml of salt to 1 L of water), or Gatorade.
2. Casualty should rest.

TREATING SHOCK

It is not unusual for a person who has incurred an injury to suffer from shock. Some of the symptoms of shock are pale, clammy skin; rapid pulse rate; rapid, shallow breathing; thirst; nausea and sometimes vomiting; feeling a lack of sufficient air; anxiety or nervousness; and confusion. (It is not shock if the person is warm and dry skinned and has good colouring.)

Once you have given first aid for the injury that caused the shock, treat the shock:

1. Place the casualty in a resting position. If there is no suspected head or spine injury and the person is fully conscious, place in the shock position—lying on the back with feet and legs raised about 30 cm. This position encourages the flow of blood to the vital organs.
2. Keep the casualty warm, handle gently and reassure often.

3. If the casualty complains of thirst, you can moisten the person's lips but don't give anything to eat or drink.
4. If there are any signs of loss of consciousness, vomiting or impaired breathing, put the casualty in a recovery position as described above. Shock can cause death, and once it has set in, it may be difficult to reverse.

FRACTURES

An open fracture is one in which the skin has broken or the broken bone is protruding through the skin. A closed fracture does not show broken skin over the injury.

Symptoms of a broken bone
1. Pain and tenderness at the point of fracture.
2. Deformity—an abnormal shape or position of a limb.
3. Swelling from blood leaking into the tissues around the break.
4. Loss of function—the person is unable to move the limb.
5. Crepitus—the sound of broken bone ends grating together.
6. Unnatural movement—the limb moves or bends in an unusual way.
7. Shock occurs commonly, but not always, with fractures.

The objective of first aid for fractures is to prevent further injury, reduce pain and minimize swelling. When in doubt, treat an injury as a fracture.

Treatment
1. If it is not cold, remove clothing to inspect the injury. If it is cold and you fear hypothermia, assess the injury but ensure that the casualty is not needlessly exposed.
2. If possible, provide first aid before moving the casualty.
3. For an open fracture, treat the wound by stopping bleeding and applying a sterile dressing. Check circulation.

4. Splint the fracture:
    (a) Any rigid material—for example, a branch—can be used as a splint. If treating a broken leg, you can use the other leg as a splint by putting padding between the legs (perhaps a rolled-up blanket) and tying legs together.
    (b) Tape pieces of material around the splint and place padding in natural hollows of the body.
    (c) Secure the splint with wide knotted bandages on either side of the fracture. Do not have knots pressing against the skin. Leave the injured area clear for observation; also leave access to fingers or toes to check for circulation. (Compare with the warmth and colour of the uninjured side. Check often.) A belt can be used for a sling if required.
5. If possible, elevate and support the injury.
6. Unless it is extremely cold, apply cold directly over the injury—but not directly on the skin—to reduce swelling.

DISLOCATION

A dislocation is the continuing separation of parts of a joint. This condition is most common in shoulders, fingers, thumbs, kneecaps and jaws. Returning the dislocated bones back into position is called reduction. Only a trained person should attempt reduction. To treat a dislocation in the wilderness:

1. Compare the injured joint with the uninjured one to determine if there is dislocation. The shoulder, as an example, will look angular as opposed to rounded, the joint may be swollen, the arm cannot move easily, and there is considerable pain.
2. Splint the injury in the most comfortable position and get medical attention as soon as possible. If the casualty has painkiller, it may be helpful.

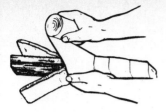

Padding a wooden splint.

Applying a splint.

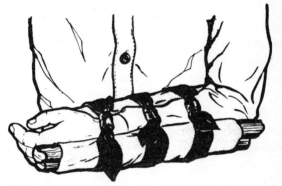

Sticks rolled in cloth to form an improvised splint for the forearm.

Gently place broken leg into line with the other. Pad well and immobilize by bandaging to the unbroken leg or to a well-padded splint reaching from the foot almost to the armpit.

SPRAIN

A sprain is a tearing or stretching of ligaments around a joint. It is recognizable by swelling and discoloration, limited use and pain. To treat, use RICE—Rest, Ice, Compression and Elevation:

1. Rest the injured person.
2. Apply cold to the injury, 15 minutes on, 15 off.
3. Apply gentle pressure with bandages to slow the flow of fluids to the injury (do not compress if the casualty has diabetes or disease of the blood vessels).
4. Raise the injured part, preferably above heart level.

CONCUSSION

Usually caused by a blow to the head or neck, a concussion is a temporary disturbance of brain function. Signs of a concussion are headache, decreasing level of consciousness, flushed face and rising temperature, vomiting, stronger or slower pulse, blurred vision, abnormal breathing pattern, changed personality (may be aggressive), twitching muscles and unequal pupil size or reaction to light. To treat:

1. Secure casualty by placing support around the neck. Place casualty in a rest position. Treat as though it is a neck injury.
2. Check often. If the casualty has difficulty breathing, check airway and use jaw thrust without head tilt to keep airway open.
3. If casualty is unconscious, carefully support head and neck and put in recovery position.
4. Treat any open wounds.
5. Do not leave casualty alone, and call for medical help.

DIARRHEA

Watery bowel movements may be the result of a change in diet and water. Purify all water (see chapter 8) and make sure that you wash your hands with soap and water before preparing or eating food. To treat:

1. Rest and fast (except for drinking water) for 24 hours.
2. Then take only liquids, such as clear soups and teas, and avoid fats, starches and sugar. Avoid fruit for a few days.
3. Eat small meals. Continue to drink lots of fluids.

HEAT EXHAUSTION

When the body becomes overheated, blood vessels in the skin dilate and the blood flow to the major organs becomes inadequate. Similar to shock symptoms, the symptoms of heat exhaustion are excessive sweating, rapid pulse and cold, clammy skin, and the casualty may complain of dizziness, blurred vision and nausea. Note: In this stage the casualty does not feel hot. Once the person feels hot, heatstroke has set in, and this is a medical emergency. To treat heat exhaustion:

1. Place casualty in a rest position with feet slightly elevated.
2. Give water or salty fluids (about 5 ml of salt to 1 L of water), as much as casualty will drink. Rehydration drinks replace salt. If there is no salt available, give water alone. Do not give alcohol or drinks containing caffeine.

HEATSTROKE (SUNSTROKE)

Heatstroke causes the body temperature to rise far above normal as a result of prolonged exposure in hot, humid conditions. It is life threatening, and its symptoms are a body temperature of 40° C or higher, noisy breathing and flushed, hot skin that can be dry or wet. The casualty will be hot to touch, with a rapid pulse that gets weaker in later stages. The casualty may be restless and may complain of headache, fatigue, dizziness and nausea, which may advance to vomiting, convulsions and unconsciousness. To treat:

1. Cool the casualty immediately. Move to shade.
2. Remove clothing and place the victim in cool water. If this is not possible, wet the casualty down (particularly on the neck, in the armpits and in the groin) and fan. Do not rub with alcohol.
3. Monitor closely. Attempt to get medical attention, since the casualty's temperature may be irregular for some time.

MUSCLE CRAMPS

Heat or muscle cramps, usually in the legs and abdomen, are caused by losing too much water and salt through sweating. They are often the result of heavy exertion in a hot environment. The casualty will complain of cramps and may sweat excessively. To treat:

1. If not severe, a leg cramp may be immediately stretched out by extending the leg and pulling the toes up towards the body.
2. Give several cups of salty fluid (5 ml salt to 1 L of water).
3. Place in rest position in a cool place.

BURNS

A burn caused by fire, scalding water, chemicals, hot food or the sun is painful, and if it is a major burn, shock can be a life-threatening result. In a first-degree burn, the skin is red, sensitive and sore, but there is no blistering; a second-degree burn is very painful, and the added symptoms are swelling, blistering and "weeping" skin; a third-degree burn may not be painful, since nerves have been destroyed, but the skin may actually be charred or whitish in appearance. Infection usually sets in after a third-degree burn, and healing is slow. To treat, follow the three Cs:

1. Cool a burn as quickly as possible. Immerse in cool water or put under running water for 10 to 15 minutes until burning pain stops. If you can't do either of the above, gently place

cool, wet cloths on the burn. In winter, you can sprinkle snow gently on the burn. Do not rub the burn. Note: When cooling a large area, beware of hypothermia. Except for the burned area, keep the casualty covered and warm.

2. Clean any minor burn with soap, rinse well and let air-dry. For serious burns, do not attempt to remove charred clothing that is stuck to the injury. Do not touch the burn or breathe or cough on it. If a hand is burned, remove rings before swelling occurs.

3. Cover the burn with a clean and, if possible, sterile bandage. Do not use flannel or woollen material. For second- and third-degree burns, secure firmly with another bandage or piece of fabric.

4. Give fluids and treat for shock. (For the best kind of fluid, combine ½ tsp salt and ½ tsp baking soda in 1 L of water and add sugar to taste.)

SNOW BLINDNESS

Caused by exposure of the unprotected eye to glare on snow, snow blindness can occur on an overcast day. It can be prevented by wearing sunglasses or goggles (see chapter 3). Symptoms are burning, irritated, itchy eyes that are sensitive to light, headaches and swollen eyelids. To treat:

1. Place the casualty in a dark or shaded area. If he or she is wearing contact lenses, they should be removed.
2. Do not allow the casualty to rub the eyes.
3. Get the casualty to rest.
4. Apply cold, wet cloths for relief of pain. If the person has painkiller, it may be taken. Snow blindness usually passes within a day or two.

FROSTBITE

Frostbite, or freezing of the body tissues, most often affects the toes, fingers and face. Surface frostbite (also called frost nip) affects only the skin and does not cause damage. Deep frostbite may cause loss of tissue and permanent damage, such as the loss of part or all of a hand or foot.

Surface frostbite is characterized by white, waxy-looking skin. The tissue beneath is still soft, and the casualty may have no pain. Symptoms of deep frostbite are cold, white (sometimes greyish-blue) skin that is numb. If the skin freezes and then thaws, there will be pain, swelling, discoloration and large blisters. To treat:

1. For surface frostbite, warm the body part. For example, place bare feet inside another person's parka to warm them. Protect the frozen area from further exposure, since it will easily freeze again.
2. For deep frostbite, use the injured part as little as possible. If it must be used to get to a camp, leave it frozen.
3. Give the casualty warmth, food and liquids. Try thawing the body part by submerging in warm (not hot) water, and try to move it slightly. Water temperature should be about 40° to 42° C.
4. Continue the thawing procedure for 20 to 40 minutes, until skin turns pink. (There may be no improvement.)
5. Put small sterile pads between injured toes or fingers and cover the injury loosely with sterile bandages.
6. Elevate the injured part and keep it warm. There must be no pressure on the injury. Get medical assistance as soon as possible. Make sure the injured area does not get frozen again.

BLISTERS

Blisters are often caused by ill-fitting boots. To prevent blisters, be aware of "hot spots" and examine your foot for redness. Apply a wide band of first-aid tape, duct tape or moleskin to the whole area to protect it from further friction. Application of tincture of benzoin around the area helps the tape adhere firmly. To treat:

1. Once a fluid-filled blister appears, cut a doughnut shape out of moleskin or tape and place it around the blister.
2. Do not burst blisters. Clean and keep covered.

SNAKE BITE

British Columbia's only venomous snake is a species of rattlesnake found in the southern Interior. Easily identified by the spade-shaped head, thick neck, thick body and blunt tail that has a rattle, rattlers seek shade during the day. Bites occur when they are touched or stepped on by accident. To prevent snake bites, don't put hands and feet in places that you cannot see, don't turn or lift rocks or fallen trees (use a stick, if necessary to move something), and don't put your sleeping bag near rock piles. Sometimes a snake bite will happen quickly, and the person may not realize it has occurred. A snake bite is identifiable by distinct fang marks (nonpoisonous bites do not have a fang imprint) and immediate sharp burning pain; swelling occurs within 5 to 10 minutes and spreads rapidly. The casualty will experience numbness and tingling of lips, face and scalp within 30 to 60 minutes of the attack. There may also be twitching of mouth and eye muscles and a rubbery or metallic taste in the mouth. These symptoms may be followed by weakness, sweating, vomiting and fainting. In 2 or 3 hours there will be bruising and, later, large blisters. A serious bite will result in breathing difficulties and collapse after 6 to 12 hours. Do not give alcohol, cut the fang marks, try to suck venom, apply tourniquet or apply cold to the injury. Treat a nonpoisonous bite by cleaning and treating as an infected wound. A tetanus injection should be given. To treat a poisonous bite:

1. Calm and place casualty at rest and keep from moving to slow spread of venom.
2. Wash the area with soap and water.
3. If possible, splint the limb to prevent movement. Check for swelling; you may have to loosen bandages.

4. Keep the injury elevated above the heart.
5. Get medical assistance.

BEE OR WASP STING

For most people, a bee or wasp sting results in a quick, sharp pain and some swelling and itching. People who have an allergic reaction to bee stings must carry a kit that includes an injectable drug (adrenaline) and pills. To treat:

1. Gently scrape the stinger off the skin using the edge of a knife. Do not take it out with fingers or tweezers, since you will squeeze more poison into the wound.
2. Apply cold to the injury by putting it in water or applying a plastic bag of water. A paste of baking soda and water soothes a bee sting; a wasp sting can be treated with juice of wild cranberries, wild rhubarb or sorrel. If there is swelling, itching and pain, antihistamines may be given according to directions.
3. If the person is allergic, you may have to assist in giving him or her medication. Watch that breathing is normal.
4. If a person shows allergic reactions—for example, difficulty in breathing, nausea and vomiting, swelling of tongue, nose and mouth, or hives—get medical assistance.

BIBLIOGRAPHY

Fears, J. Wayne. 1986. *Complete Book of Outdoor Survival*. New York: Outdoor Life Books.

Merry, Wayne. 1994. *St. John Ambulance Official Wilderness First-Aid Guide*. Toronto: McClelland & Stewart.

St. John Ambulance. 1995. *First on the Scene: St. John Ambulance Training for Life*. Ottawa: St. John Ambulance.

Szczawinski, Adam F., and Nancy J. Turner. 1978. *Edible Garden Weeds of Canada*. Ottawa: National Museums of Canada.

———. 1979. *Edible Wild Fruits and Nuts of Canada*. Ottawa: National Museums of Canada.

Turner, Nancy J. 1995. *Food Plants of Coastal Peoples*. Vancouver: UBC Press.

Wiseman, John. 1993. *SAS Survival Guide*. Glasgow: HarperCollins.

INDEX